# IF YOU COULD SEE ME

## LIFE MOTHERHOOD AND THE PURSUIT OF SANITY

## ERIN MAHONE

LEADERS IN GLOBAL PUBLISHING

Published by Motivational Press, Inc.
1777 Aurora Road
Melbourne, Florida, 32935
www.MotivationalPress.com

ISBN: 978-1-62865-490-5

# CONTENTS

## PURSUIT OF SANITY

Dear Reader,

My story is just like yours. Mundane really, there's marriage and divorce, and marriage and divorce, middle school, amputations, cars rolling over people, birth, death, sickness, hypochondria, bad hair, bi-polar disorder, enormous glasses, schizophrenia, guilt, religion, singing, laughter, tears, parenting, anxiety, Wheel of Fortune, yelling, crying, yoga, duct tape, produce, musical theatre, Vicks Vapo-rub, ADHD, drinking from the dog bowl, and so much more...I'm just like you. This selection of musings from my Life, Motherhood, and Pursuit of Sanity never feels finished, it is, like me, imperfect. Life is hard and I'm just a girl – who keeps showing up.

Much love,

Erin

BUBBE: You don't visit me enough.

ME: Bubbe, you live so far away.

BUBBE: I'm not as far away as I will be when I'm dead.

This book is dedicated to the magnificent people who taught me how to keep showing up. I love you Bubbe and Zayde.

To my parents Mom, Dad and my bonus Mom Cindy for the unconditional love, limitless support, and our untraditional family!

To my aunts, uncles, siblings, and cousins who have supported me so completely in the telling of these stories.

To Emmy for reminding me not to allow fear to stand in my way.

And of course to the people who have given me so many stories - Keith, Lulubelle, Leo, and Duckling.

# FOREWORD

I N 2006, MY BEST FRIEND (a neon artist from Roanoke, VA) died after he was blown into a power line while installing a neon sign. A month after his death, his girlfriend discovered she was pregnant. In my effort to create a care package for my friend's family, I ended up writing a one-man show called, "The Neon Man and Me."

The production toured the country seven times, including a short run off-Broadway, aired as a nationally televised PBS Special, raised a handsome sum of money for a bunch of non-profits, grew to include a public school curriculum and in the process made me sort of famous.

For the next ten years, I felt like I was sitting in the passenger seat of God's car. As he drove, I watched an unexplored new world pass outside my window and stepped onto 1,479 stages in all. Never having acted in a school play or studied theatre, I felt incredibly fortunate to be along for the ride.

Then, one night God pulled up to my east village apartment. I got out and didn't get back in. I watched the car disappear.

The thing is, the story I told.... it wasn't the story I wanted to tell. It was the story I was called to tell. It was the story that my heart told me to tell. It was the story that God wanted me to tell. But, there was another story I craved to tell more.

In the year leading up to my friend's death, I'd begun to explore what it was like growing up in a "Jewish Closet." A term I would eventually use to define a symbolic safe haven and hide-away common to second-generation Holocaust survivors like myself.

Growing up in a family of Holocaust survivor's who encouraged me to hide my identity behind the door of assimilation made the Jewish Closet very real. My mother often announced, "Don't tell anyone you are Jewish. They will find you. They will kill you. You will die." To question the closet was a form of betrayal.

I knew the time would come when I felt ready to leave my closet. By 2006, leaving was all I thought about.

This is why during the first staged-reading of "The Neon Man and Me" one reviewer said, "If this is supposed to be a story about your best friend, then why is there so much stuff in it about being Jewish?" And, he was right. The story about claiming my identity would have to wait.

In subsequent years, I would explore the topic of Jewish identity on stage. But, without a road map to guide me in dealing with the perplexing process of how my family responded to our tragic past: the PTSD, medications, addictions, violence, police stations, mental hospitals, etc., my attempts were haphazard at best.

Giving birth to a Matzo Ball on stages throughout the bible belt and doing stand-up routines dressed as Jesus were supposed to help me understand my personal struggles with the Jewish Closet. My intention was to explore the topic of identity and perhaps heal parts of my past, but I ended up making myself feel more alone and isolated in the process. I was chased off stage in Washington DC, labeled an anti-Semite in more than one synagogue, and according to my rabbi I became a good example of why mixed marriages don't work.

---

Then, in 2013 my memoir "The Bohemian Love Diaries" was released and something strange happened. Closet owners all over the world began to reach out to me. And not just Jewish Closet owners. It seemed like everyone had a secret in their family that they'd hidden in a closet. I'd created some kind of magnet with my writing that drew them to me. Many wrote emails. Many more passed by with a secret nod. Some moved into my neighborhood and never left.

One of these people was Erin Mahone. I first met her through the JCC where she works as the Director of Cultural Arts and Jewish Education. She'd asked me to come down, sign books and give a reading. Traveling to my hometown to meet Erin, I felt like I'd come full circle.

When we met, I felt a special connection; as if clandestine and filled with butterflies, though it would take years to understand the reason why.

Over the next few years, Erin kept inviting me to participate in projects and panels and podcasts and I found myself saying yes and yes and yes. I came to know Erin as a performing artist, a humanitarian, a friend and finally an author.

I wasn't aware I needed her and yet I've found that nothing could be further from the truth. As you turn the pages of "If You Could See Me" it's my hope that you'll also realize how desperate all of us are for her company.

She offers what we all wish our own mothers were able to offer us: "the majesty of imperfection" and unconditional self-acceptance.

On the page, it's impossible not to understand that she's unafraid to run away from your ugliest revelations. Sometimes being close to someone who can admit so freely that "being perfect and in control every second is the most painful part of being alive" is as close to self-medicating with ice cream as you can get. In fact, it's often better.

Through her words I am able to accept that I am both more than what I do and more than what I was. That even when I don't shine I still shine brighter; which isn't easy in a world that encourages us to remake ourselves online one status update at a time. Erin just doesn't allow it. Do-overs. Yes. Makeovers. No.

Thinking back on 2006, I now realize that the choice between two stories was never mine to make, no matter what I thought. I've since learned that we don't choose stories as much as they choose us. And as writers, we don't write stories as much as they write us.

Underneath the story about the death of my friend was a story about identity and underneath that story is yet another that shall remain hidden from the world until I'm brave enough to tell it. I'm convinced that Erin will play in an important part in how this new story is told. The wisdom and inspiration she's poured onto the pages of "If You Could See Me" assures it. Until then, I plan to spend more time with her and her words.

Erin has the ability to make space for your darkest moments without the need to pick you up off the floor, make it all better with a sandwich or turn the light on. Therapy has since helped me identify the feeling as delicious fright, which as it turns out, is the same feeling I felt when I met her. Perhaps, you dear reader will find yourself feeling the same way as you turn the page.

**Slash Coleman**
Author of *The Bohemian Love Diaries*

# LIFE

---

"Just because you're miserable,
doesn't mean you can't enjoy your life."

**~Annette Goodheart**

---

# BUBBE AND ZAYDE

PHILADELPHIA, DECEMBER 1952

A 19 year old girl gets into a cab. Behind the wheel is a fair haired, kind faced, blue eyed 26 year old veteran.

"What's your name," he asked.

"Marlene," she answered, "what's yours?"

"Lenny."

She smiled shyly as he grinned at her through the rear view mirror.

That night he proposed and two weeks later they went down to city hall. But they almost didn't get married. You see, on that first date she told him in a momentary lapse of reason, that she was 23. Only now, when they went down to fill out the paperwork she just couldn't continue her charade. She couldn't enter into their marriage with him thinking she was 4 years older than she actually was. She couldn't keep her pretend birthday straight in her head forever...

"You ok?" He asked as they sat side by side filling out the paperwork.

"I have to confess something," she said.

"Ok, what is it?"

"I'm really 21." She lied again. "What is wrong with me?!" she thought in her head.

"Ok," he said, "ok, it's ok. Anything else?"

"I'm 19."

"I can't do this – you're just a kid. It ain't right."

"It's fine," she answered calmly, "it's no big deal. I'm the same as I was 2 minutes ago. I'm the same as I was when I got into your cab."

Needless to say, they got married. But shortly after Lenny began acting strangely. He was volatile and paranoid. He was hallucinating and having delusions. Soon after, he was diagnosed with paranoid schizophrenia. Her family and his for that matter, encouraged her to institutionalize him, to move on, get married again, and pretend it never happened. But she couldn't do that. "He didn't deserve to be locked away like an animal," she would say. So they made it work. That girl and that boy were my grandparents. I called them Bubbe and Zayde. They spent 47 years taking care of each other.

My Zeyda had a prolific career as a schizophrenic. His delusions of grandeur were indeed grandiose. He spent time as an astronaut, the chauffeur for JFK during the assassination, frequently tracked in various inventive ways by the KGB, and as the Messiah or preternaturally communicating with G-d through the placement of the cigarette butts in his ashtray or reading the alignment of the stars. He would spend hours looking up at the sky or sitting alone nodding his head. Every day was an adventure.

My Bubbe would get so angry with him when he would engage in the secret rituals like cigarette butt messages to The Lord. "Stop it, Lenny!" She would yell. Even at the other end of the house, she either knew he was doing something or she was warning him in advance.

Bubbe experienced great difficulty with anxiety and depression as a result of the stress and uncertainty of Zayde's illness and shouldering the responsibility of caring for their family. Their life together was extremely difficult and came with great sacrifices. Neither of them ever gave up and they raised four amazing children, one of whom was my father. Their children went on to give them 12 grandchildren. They had a weird relationship but his illness was never a secret. They both did whatever necessary to help him to be as healthy as possible, hospitalizations, new risky treatments, and days on end in doctors' offices. Whatever it took.

When my father was a child, Zayde spent years in and out of hospitals in an attempt to find a viable treatment and medications that worked. He underwent the bad kind of Electroconvulsive therapy "shock treatments" – the archaic 1950's version, the scary drugs, nothing like what we know today. This left Bubbe alone to care for the children, the house, and earn a living providing in home childcare. She worked hard to care for her family and give her husband what he needed to survive outside of an institution.

Zayde once had a doctor, in his old age, who's name was Dijou. He saw the name written on the white coat and thought it must mean "Die Jew" and refused to go anywhere near the doctor. His distrust of "Japs" and "A-rabs" was not racism necessarily but a combination of his service in World War II, his experience as the son of Ukrainian Jewish immigrants, all intensified by the paranoia from his disease that created so many powerful enemies.

My Bubbe told me once that when Zayde was very young he felt there was something wrong and he went to discuss it with his mother who was a Jewish immigrant from the Ukraine, sickly, and fearful in the world. "Sha, sha" she would say in her thick Yiddish accent, "You're fine. Don't say these things, people will hear you. Nothing wrong." And that was that.

His greatest gift was that he was a gentle man with a big booming voice who loved to tell stories, sing songs, and play games with us. He was full of goodness, kindness and love. He would walk over to me and put his hand on top of my head as if blessing me and say "My Erin Peyton. Shaina Madel."(which means beautiful girl in Yiddish.).

Although their struggles were never a secret our grandparents and our parents often recalled about all the fun they used to have. They were always laughing and doing crazy things like rearranging the bedrooms in their tiny house in the middle of the night so everyone got a new room. Their kids' friends were always welcome and fed no matter how much they ate. They made everyone feel like a part of the family.

My dad told stories of his best friend coming over and eating the entire family's dinner before they sat down. My uncle, once invited the entire basketball team home for lunch in the middle of the school day. They both would come home in the middle of the day to watch *The Young and the Restless* with their mom and eat lunch.

My siblings and cousins and I (12 of us), would spend weekends at their house. We would eat chocolate ice cream with crushed pretzels, baked spaghetti with American cheese on top, pretzels and mustard, lox with eggs and onions. We'd play rummy tile, trivial pursuit or penny poker, and have fashion shows, or put on musical reviews.

My love of performance, and telling people what to do, is a direct result of being the oldest grandchild. On those weekends I learned to be a "Directator" creating elaborate productions, yelling at all of my cousins, doing costumes, make-up, and hair. In fact, one cousin still has a scar from the time I accidentally burned her during a hairstyling session.

Bubbe encouraged talent and vision. She made me feel like I could do anything. Unless I was doing something she didn't understand, then she wouldn't speak to me for awhile. Like the time in middle school when I was feeling fashionably adventurous and I wore Zeyda's pajamas to school. You would have thought I had kidnapped the Lindbergh baby.

I guess now I understand a little better that this reaction was partially generational but also a reflection of her incredibly high expectations for her family. Her life, though full of love, was limited as a result of Zayde's illness. She had to work so hard for everything she had that when she saw me going to 7th grade in an old man's pajamas it was just too much. She valued excellence and respected talent but she wasn't a huge fan of weirdness.

However, even though as an adult I can understand her a little better I recall that she wasn't always kind with her recriminations when you did something she didn't like or understand. The more she loved you the meaner she sometimes was in those moments. She was an incredible woman, but she wasn't perfect.

In fact, the greatest lesson she taught me is that showing up doesn't mean being perfect. She struggled with her own anger, resentment, anxiety and depression too. She yelled, blamed, gossiped, and judged, and yelled some more. There's enough material for a book on her alone – she was the center of my universe. Good, bad, otherwise she never let me down and she never let Zayde down. I can't speak for anyone else.

My grandparents would tell stories of growing up in Philly, sing us songs from their childhoods. Bubbe would sing "You are My Sunshine" or "'A' You're Adorable" and of course her amended version of "Que Sera Sera." She would sing that song to us when we were little. Her version was slightly different from the one made famous by Doris Day. She would sing "When I was just a little girl I asked my mother 'What will I be? Will I be handsome, will I be rich - *or will I just be a son of a bitch?*" Bubbe was the real comedian in the family.

Zeyda on the other hand would take out his teeth and sing "Flat Foot Floogie with the Floy Floy." He even did a little dance where he raised his right hand and pointed his index finger toward the sky. Then he would do a little shuffle kick to the side. In his low, gravely smoker's baritone and big toothless grin he was as good as any vaudevillian.

The "Flat Foot Floogie" song and dance routine is a huge part of my childhood experience. A few years ago I posed all three of my kids in front of the fireplace with their index fingers pointing up, arms raised high. I posted the picture on Facebook with a caption about how my Zayde loved to sing "Flat Foot Floogie" to us as children and we were honoring his memory. Shortly after posting, my brother called me.

"Do you know what that song means?" he asked.

"What are you talking about?" I replied. "It's gibberish. It doesn't mean anything!" I answered, annoyed that my brother was trying to ruin my sweet moment.

"Look it up." He insisted.

Begrudgingly, I did and according to Wikipedia – the most reliable source on the internet – a flat foot "floozie" with the floy floy was, in fact, a prostitute with untreated syphilis. This time, it turned out, Wikipedia was right...Awesome! Then, of course, the guys who give the Mother of the Year award showed up at my door to inform me I would never be a recipient.

Zayde had a magnificent long term memory. He remembered every street in Philadelphia, where he grew-up and drove a cab after getting out of the military. On one trip back to Philly, later in his life, he did insist that they had moved a bridge, other than that, he had perfect recall! Zayde would talk about his youth in the streets and alleyways, shooting craps with his friends, "Farty George" and "Louie Two-Legs", who incidentally drove a car and evaded police on multiple occasions even though he didn't have any legs.

We moved a lot when I was young, it was the most unstable part of my own upbringing. My parents got married and divorced a few times– only once to each other. From the time I was 2, until I was 12 there were several new step-families, new schools, split school years, new friends, new starts. There was a lot of fear, uncertainty, loneliness, and sadness during that time. Bubbe must have known, because she was always there. She always showed up.

At times when I didn't live close by she would call me most nights and we would watch *Wheel of Fortune* together over the phone. "Erin, I solved the puzzle in 4 letters! Can you believe it?!" She would exclaim in her thick Philadelphia accent. Then we would watch the rest of the show and *Jeopardy* too if we could. She's no longer here so I can't ask her all of the questions I have as a grown-up that I didn't know to ask as a kid. Did she makes those calls for me or for herself? Probably both – I knew that she needed me as much as I needed her.

Having grandchildren for Bubbe was an opportunity to start over and to be for us what Zeyda's schizophrenia, poverty, depression, and circumstance prevented her from being for her own children. Grandchildren gave her a second chance. She made the absolute most of it.

Most years, on New Year's Eve, there was some collection of grandchildren spending the night at their house. We would watch Dick Clark's New Year's Rockin' Eve, with most of America. Utter, child-focused pandemonium was the evening's agenda. Disney movies, music, running, dancing, and food would happen. But 5 minutes before midnight, she would gather us all in the family room in front of the TV. She and Zayde would run into the kitchen and gather every pot, pan, lid, and wooden spoon in the house and distribute two to every child. We would stand in breathless anticipation, in front of the television, and wait for the countdown. Together we would shout:

"10...9...8...7...6...5...4...3...2...1... HAPPY NEW YEAR!!!!!"

We would bang our pots and pans together ringing in the New Year with joy and excitement for the good things to come. Banging and yelling in the family room was not enough for Bubbe, at 12:01 she would throw open the back door and send us out into the front yard to continue the celebration for all of the neighbors to see. All of us standing on the front lawn as the New Year began in our pajamas and sock feet yelling and running with complete elation is one of the greatest memories of my childhood. Bubbe and Zayde had a way of making everything special.

They drove each other crazy, my grandparents, fighting and bickering almost constantly. Despite it all, they managed to stay married for 47 years through poor health, mental instability on both their parts, child bearing and rearing, money troubles, and whatever else life served up. They taught me the art of compassion, humility, and most importantly, finding a way to smile through life's shittiest situations.

I often think about all the instances of violence and incarceration that happen when people with mental illness are misunderstood. In many cases those individuals don't have strong support systems, loving families, or wives like my Bubbe telling them exactly what to do every moment. I know how easily that could have been my Zeyda's fate. He was diagnosed at a time when it would have been perfectly acceptable and reasonable for Bubbe to put him away, or just leave but she didn't. They spent 47 years taking care of each other.

So many people struggle to understand their mental illness and along that journey many encounter violence, discrimination, or worse. I have always felt so sad for Zayde having to go so many years without getting help before he found Bubbe. I cannot imagine the fear and confusion of experiencing the onset of schizophrenia all alone with nowhere to turn. 65 years ago people were afraid of what would happen to them if they asked for help. This is the primary motivation for my writing, performing, and advocacy. I hope that the more we share our stories, the fewer people will have to live with that fear and shame.

There are those who will say "They wouldn't want you to tell these stories. They wouldn't want you to reveal so much about their lives." To them I say – if it meant being better understood, if it meant not being afraid to tell people what was really going on – if it meant feeling less pain, loneliness, and isolation – they would pay me to tell it.

They would approve. They did approve. They wanted me to do this. They loved me and they wanted their story heard. They wanted their pain to have meant something.

They would want the world to know the wonderful things too.

Were there terrible things? Yes. Aren't there always terrible things, in everyone's lives? Yes. Am I lying by dwelling on the positives? No, I'm sharing the wonderful.

The truth is, I am an adult and I *choose* to remember the fun and hilarity as much as possible. It keeps me hopeful. I put the pain in the 'do something' box, in the songs that I sing, in my passion for advocacy, and in my motivation to tell these stories.

By telling them, we reduce the stigma, we are saying that all people have worth, gifts, love to offer. Everyone deserves a chance, even if they need more help, more support, and if necessary, medication to make it happen.

# A MOTHER'S LOVE - THE PRODUCE STORY

A MOTHER'S LOVE IS A STRANGE and wondrous thing. It is something one can never fully understand until they become a mom themselves. In the name of love and concern for their children's wellbeing, parents lose all sense of what is sane and reasonable...if they're good parents of course.

At 22 years old, after years of talking about it, I decided to move to New York City. But in my super flakey fashion I just packed a bag, some shoes, my make-up, and a papasan chair cushion and left. I serendipitously secured a job and I was on my way. A friend offered up her floor until I could get settled and that's how it all started. Practically overnight, I had a whole new life.

After almost a month on the floor I found an apartment with some friends. I called my parents excited to share the news and they began immediately making plans to get my stuff out of the house and up to me. Early one Sunday morning, my family packed up a U-Haul and drove my stuff to my new apartment. They dropped it all off, ate some pizza, turned around and drove right back to Virginia.

I spent the day and night unpacking. The next morning I went to work as usual. When I came home, one of my roommates said my mother had called and she sounded extremely upset and that I should call her immediately! Now this was not surprising to me because, you see, my mother always sounds upset when she is on the phone. She speaks as if she is on fire "HELLO!" to which the person on the other end, now panicked, would say "Are you ok?" and she responds still yelling, "YES, WHY?!" confused by the nature of the question. My roommates, unaccustomed to this phone manner, are filled with a sudden sense of urgency to find me and have me call her back.

I didn't rush to call her back because I'd been there before. This was my normal. I did eventually call her that night and I was surprised to find that she really was upset. In a hysterical, frantic, and very high pitched voice she said, "Erin, I realized when I got home last night that I left behind this entire cooler filled with produce that I bought you before we left!" I waited a beat making sure I'd heard correctly. Slowly, and a little confused I replied, "It's ok mom, they have produce here."

"But I bought all this for you! So this is what we're going to do, your stepfather has a client going back to Italy tomorrow. She will fly from Richmond and layover at La Guardia. She has agreed to bring the produce with her, all you have to do is meet her at the airport to pick it up! Can you do that?!"

Again, confused, "Drive over an hour to the airport to pick up produce when there's a Whole Foods a few blocks away?"

"Uh-huh."

"No."

"Oh..."

"REALLY!!! This sounds reasonable to you?" I thought to myself.

"No Mom. I think it'll be ok. Really. We have perfectly good supermarkets up here. Don't worry."

She started to cry. "Blbblblblbl"

"I love you too. I have to go now."

"Bblblblbl."

I hung up. At equal levels I was confused, hysterical laughing, and irritated. I wasn't a mom yet and clearly didn't understand. In my mind, she was just simply insane; now let's not downplay the crazy - for it is one of her most charming qualities. But now as a mom myself, with my own brand of crazy, I totally get it.

Life is messy and motherhood follows that model. We aren't perfect - no matter how hard we try to be. We often make mountains out of molehills like obsessing over produce when really we're just trying to say "I want to make sure you have everything you need." My mom reached the point where she couldn't do that anymore. I had grown up and she was trying to figure out what that meant for us - together, and as individuals. What do you do when there's nothing you can do? Cry over produce, of course.

---

"Suddenly he knew what was so special about mothers. She looked at him smiling, and said, 'I'll love you to the ends of the universe.'"

**~ "Milo", *Mars Needs Moms* by Berkeley Breathed**

---

Growing up with my mom was an experience to say the least. The complex sea of mother/daughter relationship challenges was made all the more challenging by her bi-polar disorder and obsessive compulsive tendencies. The 80's and 90's were filled with therapy, weekend workshops on rage with pillow punching and other activities that I would half listen to her describing. We were raised on pop psychology buzz words about "old tapes": our faulty thoughts based on past experiences which inform our present and future decisions; "our inner child", and "doing work". There was lots of talk about boundaries – which for me was mostly about the cat and not "crashing the cat's boundaries" which translated to "don't pick up the cat when he doesn't want to be picked up."

Living with mom required analyzing every miniscule detail of our lives, every decision, interaction, and option. This made me self-aware – a positive quality - and was exceedingly overwhelming – not so positive. In my work, the reality of growing up like that has made me exceptionally perceptive of other people's needs, wants, and desires. I can anticipate any eventuality because when I was a kid I never knew who I was going to meet when I woke up each day. Would there be a cheerful, fun lady? The woman who was insightful, spiritual, and wise? The woman who encouraged me to be strong and independent? Or the mom who rarely left her bedroom for a year?

Mom and I are making our way through this life together. It's rocky and filled with frustration, but we are each other's greatest champions. I will never give up hope or lose faith in her ability to rebound. But I also remain vigilant and realistic. It's a very difficult balance and I never feel as if I'm getting it right.

My mother has the greatest laugh. When she's in the hole – that's how we affectionately refer to her depression – she doesn't laugh. I have a Pavlovian response to her laughter because at the very deepest level it is my greatest comfort. When mom is laughing it means everything is ok, even if just for today.

My mom has significant trauma from a very broken relationship with her mother. She is so hurt and so beaten down by this toxic relationship that it has damaged her ability to develop and maintain healthy relationships. She has been diagnosed with everything under the sun but mostly she lives with the bi-polar diagnosis. She wants and needs to explore and face her trauma and yet she has not been able to find a treatment that helps her find the peace she so desperately seeks. She finds some success with medication but they don't treat the impact of emotional trauma, they just help her get out of bed most of the time. Even in the past when she tried to find effective treatments, while also working and raising us kids she never found any real solutions – unless you can count the temporary kind that were reflected through the eyes of a man or the needs of her children. Sadly, those were always more of a distraction than a solution.

The pain and helplessness that is experienced as the child of a parent struggling with mental illness cannot be described in words. It's very personal – really, really personal. It is a mixture of fear, uncertainty, loneliness, anger, confusion, disappointments, compassion, patience and frustration. You never know the right thing to do, nothing you do really works, you always feel like if somehow you were different then things would be different for them, you feel sad and hurt for them and also angry and hurt for yourself. It is maddening. Children know when their parents are really in pain – really struggling – and it messes with their perceptions of the world. It makes everything feel unsafe, uncertain, and lonely.

"I just want peace," my mother says whenever she has the chance. To which I respond, "I don't know that I've met many people who dream of a life of chaos and misery." After her most recent hospitalization I traveled to her home in Florida. She had celebrated her 60th birthday by ending a relationship she thought would become a marriage. She had moved down there to start a new life and instead, everything fell apart. Things had been pretty hard for a number of years leading up to the move and I was afraid but equally hopeful that this would be the fresh start she needed. It is true what they say – when you move away you can't leave yourself behind.

When she got out of the hospital I went down for the weekend to help her find a new place to live and get settled. She was committed to staying down there. She didn't want to return home, to Virginia, in failure. She wasn't ready to give up. That's the thing about my mom – she doesn't give up easily. One night during that weekend we lay in my hotel room bed talking and laughing, a lot. She was so happy to have me there. I was afraid and uncertain of the right thing to do for her. As we lay there in the dark getting close to sleep, after a successful day of finding her a lovely place to live – she spoke that famous line again.

"I just want peace, Erin."

"I know mom. Life is hard, finding peace is a choice we have to make all the time, and some days it's all we can do not to drink ourselves to death."

# ON MY LAST LEG - PART 1

A T 65 YEARS OLD, my Bubbe lost her leg. After years of poor health, morbid obesity, diabetes, quadruple bypass surgery, high blood pressure, and heart disease, a tiny cut to a toe resulted in the loss of an entire leg. She spent what felt like an eternity on death's door, weeks in the hospital. She developed bed sores that were indescribable, floated in and out of consciousness, struggled, fought, and ultimately recovered miraculously.

When we first started dating my now husband and I spent a lot of time laughing and picking on each other. He didn't always know where the line was and had made a reputation for himself as the guy who could say anything and everyone would love him for it. That's a skill you know- not getting punched in the face. Sometimes he would cross over into inappropriate territory... sometimes actually try most of the time.

One day we got a call that Bubbe was in the hospital again so we went over to visit. Now Keith hadn't spent a lot of time in hospitals in his life but for me St. Mary's hospital in Richmond was kind of like a second home. However, my wisecracking man, suddenly went from being irreverent to respectful and demure in a split second upon entering the hospital. I guess that was his line.

Never knowing what to expect, we walked into her room quietly and found Bubbe in her bed napping with the TV on. I walked to her bedside and put my hand on her arm. Her eyes fluttered open and she smiled at us. I kissed her wonderfully soft cheek and said, "Hi, Bubbs" as I usually did. She said, "Hi darling," Keith piped in with a quiet "How 'ya doin'?" To which she replied, "(cough) Well, the doctor says I'm on my last leg,"

Badump bump ching.

She made these jokes all the time. Were they to mask the pain? Probably, no one wants to lose their leg at 65 years old. No one wants to suffer with ill health. What she did was put everyone at ease with humor - including herself. There is often nothing we can do about where we are as the time for preventative action has passed, so to accept our circumstances we find the funny. Whether or not she had made peace with the difficulty of losing a leg remained to be seen – but she had something in her that said, "I will not let this defeat me."

She didn't get a prosthetic leg, nor did she walk again yet she still managed to keep her house, cook for anyone who would eat, tell stories, and even drive a few times. She was an amazing and inspirational person. Her life was hard from beginning to end but she honored the path and the strength it took to get through the challenges by keeping her sense of humor. She taught me how to fold hospital corners, change the words to the old standards to make them dirty, to cook delicious food on a budget, to love with my whole heart, not to take bullshit from anyone, and to laugh when things are falling apart.

"Life is difficult, the Buddha taught, and it becomes more difficult when we struggle with it. There is no end to challenge. Not everything needs to get solved today."

**Sylvia Boorstein**

# FOR ALL ETERNITY

A CCORDING TO JEWISH LAW when a person undergoes amputation the severed appendage must be buried. So following Bubbe's surgery the arrangements were made and her leg was placed in the plot that had been purchased for her and Zayde years before.

The following year, on the day of Zayde's funeral he was laid to rest above the buried leg. He had suffered a whirlwind encounter with cancer, decades of emphysema, multiple heart attacks, and a lifetime battle with schizophrenia. On that day, after the services at the funeral home and the cemetery I sat in the car with Bubbe. We rode in silence for awhile maybe reflecting on the events of the day, the last few months, perhaps contemplating the life to come - a life without him. When all of a sudden she piped up saying, "You know it gives me great pleasure to know that for all eternity my foot is gonna be up his ass." What does it say about our family that this was not in the least bit surprising to hear come from my grandmother's mouth?

I need to clarify though - this statement was made in jest... sort of. Mourning the passing of both of my grandparents are some of the fondest memories I have. Not because I was happy that they were gone - quite the contrary - it was devastating but the week following their deaths were spent celebrating their lives. We ate, sang, laughed, some argued a little, but overall we enjoyed each other - their four children and 12 grandchildren -

the family that they created - as well as cousins, siblings, friends, and community members. We are a family that triumphs through great trials and complexity.

So as we drove away that fateful day and said our goodbyes looking toward the future, us without our beloved Zayde and father; her without this man who for better and worse she'd shared most of the last 50 years with - we knew that he was laughing at what she'd said and smiling down on us all.

---

"I don't trust anyone who doesn't laugh"

**Maya Angelou**

---

# ON MY LAST LEG – PART DEUX

WHEN MY HUSBAND'S FATHER died suddenly on the evening of September 11, 2002 while jogging in the park with his wife - we were all left unsure of how to make sense of it. Even now all these years later - it's difficult to find the words to describe the shock of that phone call informing my husband that his father was gone. It was seven months before our wedding. It's unfathomable as a parent that he's missed all of these amazing milestones, our wedding, home purchases, businesses, the birth of 5 grandchildren, and so much more.

Yet, when I think back to the time immediately following his passing there is a warmth that I cannot explain. It is when we are faced with such unbelievable and unfortunate circumstances that we find out what our relationships and the people we love are really made of.

The family honored his memory with parties - not just one. There was a memorial and an "Irish Wake". There was drinking, laughing. Everyone remembered this remarkable man, flaws and all, with joy, love, and lots of good wine. Exactly the way he would have wanted it! And those were just the big parties - not including the times that we, the family, sat around together laughing, drinking, and telling stories. There was the time when his sons were fighting over a half gallon of ice cream and he threw it in the woods, or the time he screamed at his son when he couldn't find his hammer and the boy replied "It's in your hand, Dad!!" Then there was the time that the children nearly fell off a mountain so that he could take the perfect picture of them climbing it. These stories remain at the crux of the man's legacy. They are told and retold with the surprise and awe that some stories never grow tiresome.

My father-in-law was not a religious man so it was a quandary just how the memorial service would be done. Who would preside and what would they say? Somewhere in the whirlwind of planning, consoling, contacting, writing obituaries, and making burial arrangements - with several days of sleep deprivation - it was suggested that I lead the memorial service because I "used to be an actress." Which made perfect sense to everyone. Ok sure?!

With great trepidation I took on the task of leading the memorial service for this man whose funeral was standing room only. He was truly loved. I blubbered my way through and introduced person after person who felt compelled to speak in honor of his memory. It was a magnificent experience although not the way I envisioned that I would have been meeting my husband's extended family and his parents' friends. An old Yiddish proverb, or Woody Allen, once said "we plan, and God laughs," so very true.

---

"We are all faced with a series of great opportunities brilliantly disguised as impossible situations."

**Charles Swindoll**

---

It was my father-in-law's wish to be cremated and have his ashes spread over the Chesapeake Bay. His wife decided on a compromise – after all, in marriage that is a requirement. Half of him was kept to be scattered in the Bay and the other half was entombed in a cemetery so that there would be a place to visit, and for her to be interred upon her death.

Nearly a week following his death, after the memorial service and prior to the Irish Wake at their home in Virginia Beach, Keith and I went to the funeral home to acquire the ashes. We pulled up, still in a haze, and went inside. Keith met the receptionist with a smile and stated "Hi my name is Keith Mahone and I'm here to pick up my father." The woman appeared a little puzzled and looked around to see if there was indeed someone waiting to be picked up. She didn't say anything and then Keith, understanding the misunderstanding, spoke up stating "He's been cremated." The response to which was a lot of uncomfortable bowing and apologizing. They then returned with a small cardboard box and a red velvet bag with a gold drawstring - which Keith has always affectionately referred to as the Crown Royal bag. All in all a fairly strange interaction that was nothing less than hilarious to recall during the 2 hour drive from Richmond to the beach – and of course to recount to any and all who would listen.

That weekend we paid our final respects in the way that you do following the passing of a close loved one. There wasn't much crying though. It was as if his sons and his wife were beyond crying. So Instead we walked on the beach, told stories, drank his best wine, and may, or may not, have placed his ashes in the bay, I plead the 5th.

When the party at the beach was done we made our way up I64 to Richmond and the cemetery. It was meant only for the immediate family. Keith, his brother and sister-in-law, his step-mother, and his aunt and I made our way to the place where the remainder of the ashes would be laid to rest. No one knew what to do that day. His ashes were placed in a lovely marble box which Keith and his brother lovingly compared to a car battery as it matched one in size and weight. We all stood there looking at it for a moment.

As much as everyone tried to be somber and as much as we were all filled with the finality of the events taking place - the boys couldn't stop wise cracking. They decided that they should carry the tiny box, together, the three and a half feet from the bench to the space where it would be sealed - as if they were pallbearers. We could not control our giggles at the ridiculousness of this sight! Two 6' tall, grown men, in their 30's dressed in their dark suits and ties, sweating in the Indian summer of mid-September, delicately carrying their father's marble box of ashes to its final resting place in a wall. The boys' aunt was clearly annoyed at our complete disregard for the seriousness of the occasion. She simply didn't understand and we could never have explained. We clearly were bucking all of *her* traditional funeral expectations. She huffed a few more times but voiced no more complaints. How surprised could she really be when less than a week prior - the fiancee of the dearly departed's younger son had presided over the memorial service simply because she *used to be an actress?*

When "it" was done and there were no more plans to be made, no more *"on the 11th day of September in the year 2002 our father and husband was carried away on a golden chariot into the heavens to meet his..."*, no more wine or parties to dull the quiet left in his absence, we all went out for ice cream. I'm pretty sure he would have approved.

I realize that everyone has their own way of mourning, approaching anguish, and honoring their moments of despair. My grandparent's battles with ill health and my father-in-law's passing – in addition to so many other low points in my life and in my life with my husband – were, I feel, opportunities to make something good out of the senseless and confusing lot doled out by the universe. Some may feel that this approach is disrespectful and in some cases they may be right but here everyone was laughing together. We weren't poking fun at any person or circumstance that they wouldn't have made light of themselves.

My father-in-law's passing was as tragic and unexpected as nearly anything that has occurred in our lives. We have continued to pay respect to his memory every day since then by talking about him, remembering him to our children, and honoring the legacy that he left behind. We would gladly hand over all the world's riches to have him here. Yet, the experience of his death brought everyone closer because of their willingness to cry, and yes laugh together; to share in the real emotions of things that make us know we are alive. I thank my grandparents for instilling in me the gift of humor and my father-in-law for doing the same – whether he meant to or not – for his son. And I thank the universe for making sure that we found each other.

---

"If you don't like something change it; if you can't change it, change the way you think about it."

**~Mary Engelbreit**

---

# INFINITE POWER

---

"An individual has not started living until he can rise above the narrow confines of his individualistic concerns to the broader concerns of all humanity."

**Martin Luther King Jr.**

---

I'M LUCKY. I was raised by broken people. We're all broken – every last magnificent, flawed one of us. Yet so many of us try to hide it. I know I do! Showing my flaws is really hard for me. Not being perfect and in control every second is the most painful part of being alive for me. It's a battle and I'm working on it. There have been so many opportunities in my life where I've seen the majesty of imperfection, of royally screwing up: forgetting all the words to songs mid-performance, being run over by a car in my high school parking lot, overdrawing my checking account, running out of gas, not getting a job I wanted, falling down in public – I once fell off of a bus in an evening gown!

There have been a lot of moments when I was deeply imperfect and felt I had literally nothing to offer the world. In fact, several of my young adult years were spent feeling completely lost and useless. I had to get a reasonable distance from myself to finally remember what I had been shown my entire life - no matter how many times we screw up, everyone has the ability to do something important.

My Bubbe, even though she lost her mother as a child and her father was not a nice man, her husband was diagnosed with schizophrenia - somehow she knew her own power. She was able to use what she had at her disposal to make the world better. She was warm, loving, the most unbelievable cook, funny, open-minded, meticulous, accepting, a great listener, amazing storyteller, a hard-ass, highly judgmental, and demanding. She was also generous. When she had little to give. She welcomed people into her home, fed them, loved them, cared for their children, gave whatever she had to give to help lighten their burden even though hers was plenty heavy.

And everyone worshipped her. She was not wealthy or formally educated - she was just a real person. You always knew where you stood with her. If she was mad at you - she told you. If something you said was ridiculous she made sure you were aware. I still miss her everyday.

My mother is the same way - though they are not related by blood, Bubbe is my father's mother, they share the same generosity of spirit. Mom was always taking in strays - most times they were animals but sometimes they were people. A few were my friends, whose home lives were difficult my mom welcomed them into the chaotic, messy fray of our home until fires were dampened and families could reconcile. She still does this: making a lasagna for the young mechanics who recently fixed her car, inviting over a recently divorced single dad giving him cooking lessons so he could cook for his kids, helping the single mom across the street suffering from mental illness, taking care of an elderly neighbor with no family.

These women have taught me compassion by example. Additionally, they taught me the most valuable lesson any person could ever learn: no matter how little we have or how little we think of ourselves – we still possess great power. The power to: take a moment to listen, to ask a person how they are, make a phone call, send a text message, offer to make a meal, volunteer your time, bake cookies, donate food, compliment someone's earrings – it really doesn't matter but showing others that you see them, that you care is powerful. Maybe Bubbe and mom understood this because they had experienced the pain of being invisible at points in their lives.

When I spent time working with kids as an in-home clinician – kids who were at risk of being taken from their families and whose history was always traumatic – my focus was often on giving them the opportunity to do something for someone else. For some it might be counter intuitive – they are the kids who are most in need, right? True, but also they are often kids who feel the most powerless and think they have nothing to offer. If they can feel the might that comes from doing for others they can see their own worth. Some of the most generous people I have ever encountered are those who have the least in terms of wealth or material possessions. They see the value of time and genuine concern for others.

Recently, I attended a National Philanthropy Day luncheon where people were being honored for their years of service to the community both financially or through their time and dedication to organizations in our community. I have come to realize, that even though my people didn't necessarily have wings or buildings named for them they showed us the power of service. Their love for the people in their lives and at times people they didn't know made a huge difference. They set an example for their children and grandchildren that the most powerful we can ever be is when we are in service to each other.

# IT RUNS IN THE FAMILY: TALES FROM OTHERNESS

---

"Our anxiety does not come from thinking about the future, but from wanting to control it."

**Kahlil Gibran**

---

A ND THEN OF COURSE THERE'S ME. Don't think for a second that I would get out of this family unaffected – or unafflicted for that matter. Does anyone ever feel like they are a part of the world or are we all just trying desperately to make ourselves feel less alone, less misunderstood, less like an outcast?

I have to share with you the sad and unfortunate truth that I was a weird, ugly child. I had enormous glasses and crooked teeth. My fashion sense, which developed early, looked like, well, let's just say I looked like the love child of Punky Brewster and Steve Urkel! I had the attention span of a fly but girls weren't diagnosed with ADHD back then so I didn't do so hot in school. I wrote elaborate stories, plays, and spent whole days alone in my room creating worlds. I sang constantly which was my defining characteristic. I could sing. I could barely walk without falling down due to the adult sized feet attached to my child sized body – but I could sing.

A few years ago we found a video of the 5<sup>th</sup> grade chorus concert where I had my first solo. That morning I dressed in my mother's white blouse, a long black skirt, and a broach. Why was I wearing a broach? Another one of life's unanswerable questions! I was initially placed on the very back row of the risers, where the tall kids stand. When it was my turn to solo, I stepped down from my position between the Lurch twins and sang my part. I sounded like an angel...I looked like an alien-but that's neither here nor there. When I finished I stepped to the side of the stage, at the end of the risers on the floor. Just to my right is another boy from my class, also standing on the floor he came up to my elbow.

At my mother's third wedding – yes third - the summer before 7th grade a colleague of my new step-father thought I was 25.

By 13, 8th grade, I got braces. I always had either a botched perm – thanks mom – or a really bad haircut – usually my fault as I had either cut it myself OR requested a really stupid haircut. I basically did everything I could to assist Mother Nature with what she had already blessed me with – ugliness. And as I've mentioned previously, I fell down a lot.

When you grow-up ugly, do you ever grow out of it?

I was odd, clumsy, goofy looking, super sensitive, and really creative. The world wasn't built for people like me. I have always wondered if everyone feels this way - even the pretty people. The ones who are born perfect and don't have to cultivate it – at least not on the outside. Even models talk about how they were ugly – it's never true but can it be that everyone feels out of place?

I spent inordinate amounts of time with my old Jewish grandparents as a child and adolescent so I listened to Frank Sinatra, watched black and white movies, went to the theatre, and watched Dan Rather every night at 6 pm.

You see I always knew I was weird, strange, different, talented but odd. Kids ignored me. I didn't get bullied, just ignored. We moved all the time so I never knew if that was because I was the new kid, or if it was my odd Yiddish references, or my encyclopedic knowledge of the TV Guide. I knew it was something but I couldn't put my finger on it. Still as with most children I felt ok with myself through elementary school.

We moved again the summer before 6th grade and I started middle school not knowing a single person. That began what I would like to call a slow downward spiral which I did not emerge from until I was about 22. The cute quirkiness became outright unacceptable and to mask the real me I put on a developmentally appropriate façade that was completely antithetical to my true self and deeply self-destructive.

I have always struggled with pretty debilitating anxiety. I spent years trying to mask it by pretending that nothing mattered. I wouldn't accept help or suggestions from anyone – because that would mean I was found out. So I dragged myself along, always trying to look like I knew exactly what I was doing. I was always disappointed in myself.

When I got married and had kids I could no longer justify being disappointed. I pulled myself together and white knuckled it for 10 years: finishing college, developing a new career, getting back to performing after several years absence. I worked really hard to reinvent – or invent myself – to become someone I could be proud of. And here I am.

As a mother, it's no different – with every breath I worry that my children do not have what they most need. I worry that I've not given enough at temple, at school, to charity.

I fear that our discipline is not effective, the children aren't eating enough vegetables, playing enough, playing too much. Will they get into college? Are they safe? Are they too sheltered therefore not developing their independence?

My mind is an endless loop of what ifs, maybes, and shoulds. I take deep breaths and try to stay as far away from parenting books as possible, and yet here I am constantly filled with guilt and fear for not having all the answers to every possible question.

Terrible anxiety has always made me feel as if I should be perfect every second – I don't know about you, but I'm not perfect so that is a really hard place to live.

It wasn't until I began the journey of writing my stories, owning my imperfections, challenging myself to find humor whenever possible in the painful, and at times ridiculous manifestations of my anxiety, that I was able to begin healing. Also, the right medication has been very helpful.

This work is never done. I am better than I was but I am still working toward a good, consistent emotional balance. The thing that I have realized through the course of writing and speaking about my anxiety and depression is that I am not alone. We are not alone and that has been immensely comforting.

# HOLDING IT ALL TOGETHER WITH DUCT TAPE

WHEN I FIRST BEGAN WORKING in Human Services I got a part-time job with a wonderful organization, doing great work with fantastic people. I had been a screw-up for so long that I had a lot to prove, to myself mostly, but to everyone else on earth as well, or so I thought at that time. I always said yes to new projects, stayed late, tried to have new and innovative ideas, and I never knew if any of it was working. All of my colleagues were very experienced, intelligent, and just generally intimidating. I really loved it there and wanted to feel like a valued member of the team.

Just as we were entering into the big advocacy season right before the General Assembly was to convene I was coordinating meetings and trying to get people involved in the process of self-advocacy. This was very important to everyone in the department and for everyone we served. And I was the new kid with something to prove.

On the morning of a particularly big meeting I felt it was important for me to look very professional. Most of the time we were a pretty casual office - but on that day I dressed up. I had recently bought some new clothes that I was very excited about as is generally the case with new clothes. So I decided on a particularly fabulous pair of black slacks that made my legs look super long and my butt look small...er. I paired it with a really cool fleur de lis print blouse. The choice was made, this was what I was wearing. The only problem was my bra choices for this particular shirt were limited because they were all lace which created lines under the shirt. Not good.

The only bra I had that didn't do this was one that was a few years old and from before I was a mother of two who breastfed and had some understandable weight fluctuations. In a fit of desperation I put the thing on, went down to the tool box, pulled out the duct tape, and taped those suckers up. Yes, I did it and you would have too! All day long the girls stood at attention. I felt like a million bucks with my new clothes, my important meeting, and my very perky boobs.

The day wore on and it came time to set up for the "event". I pulled out all the supplies, handouts, refreshments, and loaded them onto a cart. But first there was a huge stack of papers that I had to carry upstairs to the room we were using that night. I got onto the elevator carrying all my stuff in front of me and met up with two of the women in my department. They rode up with me. We were talking about the day when all of a sudden one of them got a strange look on her face and said in a voice that felt extremely loud - "Do you have duct tape on your boobs?!?"

I look down to see that my shirt had come undone from the pile that I was carrying and there they were for all to see. I only vaguely recollect what happened next as it is shrouded in a veil of humiliation. I blushed vigorously, explained that I obviously needed to go bra shopping, all while frantically buttoning my shirt and carrying a 6" stack of papers.

My co-worker, with whom I have since become very good friends, stated "Now that brings new meaning to holding it all together with duct tape."

I was the butt of many a joke and snicker that night from those two women. But the meeting went very well. I proved my worth and my vulnerability all at once.

The next day a select few dropped by my office to share a light jab that in the end made me feel more like a part of the team. A few weeks later, on my 30th birthday, I arrived to find my entire office covered in duct tape and I laughed all day.

I find that so much of my life has been spent trying to look like I've got it all together and often I do appear that way - but whether literally or figuratively - so often I really am just holding it all together with duct tape. But I haven't done that again and I did pay Victoria's Secret a visit very soon after this incident. Just in case you were wondering.

UPDATE: This story took place in 2007. In January 2016 – I had no choice but to employ this tactic once again. This time, with one more kid and a much bigger job I did not make a trip to Victoria's Secret and I am without shame. Life is hard, do what you can with what you have. I'll buy a new bra as soon as my kids graduate from college...I never claimed to have things figured out.

---

"Treat people as if they were what they ought to be, and you help them to become what they are capable of being."

**Johann Wolfgang von Goethe**

---

# LESSONS LEARNED WHILE TRAPPED UNDER A CAR...

WHEN I WAS 16 YEARS OLD I was being an idiot and I got hurt. To be specific, I sat on top of my friend's car, fell off, and got run over. I spent half an hour under the car, some time on the Medivac helicopter, a week in the hospital, 2 months in a hospital bed set-up in the family room, and 6 weeks in a wheelchair from a pelvic fracture – actually 5 fractures. Doctors weren't sure if I would be able to have children and I certainly scared the color out of my mother's hair. And all on my Bubbe's birthday no less...

This was a difficult and painful experience that resulted in the loss of friendships, lots of social angst, AND the full function of my body, for awhile. It left permanent scars both physical and emotional, and while it is my high school legacy, as much as all of the theatre that I did, I have never really talked about it. It's not a secret and I've told people it happened but I don't really talk about it – what it meant, and how having a near death experience before you're really old enough to understand what that means - can impact the rest of your life.

I spend a fair amount of my life – when not wifing, mothering, working, writing, or performing – thinking about how to find humor in pain, making the most of terrible situations, and continuing the process of becoming. It took me years to make any real sense of the ridiculousness of being run over by a car in the school parking lot after play rehearsal in 11th grade. As an adult I've been able to get a little perspective. As I grew further and further away from this terrible experience I began to realize that life is so fleeting and there is no sense in spending it on distractions. There is so much to be done, so much for which to be thankful, and every single circumstance we face provides an opportunity to learn something about ourselves. When I was 16 I couldn't see these things, but one day in my mid-30's I was lying in my bed when things in my life were particularly difficult and I decided that I needed a reminder of just how strong I was and what I have overcome. I made a list.

1. **Don't get trapped under a car.** (On this, I think we can all agree.)

2. **Don't sit on the hood of a car and fall off.** (Or, don't be a reckless idiot.)

3. **Once under the car try to find the bright side.** (If you're a crazy person like me you immediately start cracking jokes to put other people at ease – who cares that you are mangled, broken and your sweater is strangling you to the point of losing consciousness, it's more important that the people helping you are entertained...)

4. **Be grateful you're alive.**

5. **Be grateful you're not under the tires.** (Things can always be worse)

6. **Accept help.** (As if you had a choice.)

7. **Freaking out does not make things better.**

8. **If you get through this everything else will seem small.**

9. **Accept responsibility for finding yourself in this predicament.**

10. **Do whatever is necessary to never be here again.**

11. Because life lessons don't come in perfectly round numbers. **Don't use this as an excuse to be afraid.** Life is a series of terrifying choices and sometimes you will end up "under the car" but other times, most times, you won't. You don't always end up where you thought you would; but you always end up exactly where you're supposed to be.

---

"You can't be brave if you've only had wonderful things happen to you."

**Mary Tyler Moore**

---

# MOTHERHOOD

# DEAR ME IN 2003

D EAR ME IN 2003, welcome to motherhood! This amazing gift that you have dreamed about your entire life has finally arrived. You have never in your life felt more love, fulfillment or excitement than you will on this journey. The snuggles, baby smell, milestones, hilarious and thoughtful moments will go unmatched. This will be good – great – magical.

It is important for you to remember all of the above when you want to unleash a can of whoop-ass on your entire family. Because in addition to all of aforementioned awesomeness – the can of whoop-ass thing will happen too...a lot. I know, you can't imagine this being the case – 1 week into first time motherhood it seems impossible that every second won't feel like magic. Well suck it up sister – you've got to put on your big girl pants – this parenting thing isn't for wusses. Sh*t's about to get real!

Remember when you gave up your life as a professional actor/singer but you knew it would be ok because you would sing for your babies? Well try not to be upset when they tell you to stop singing – you're hurting their ears, and stop using those voices when you read them stories, just use your regular voice, and no we don't want to play anymore theatre games mommy – it's enough already! They love you regular – your talents mean nothing to them. Really – just you meeting their needs is the only thing that matters to them – yes, they really are that selfish – prepare yourself. This isn't about you.

You know how you think you are never going to do anything wrong as a parent and in return your children will be perfect? Well, and I mean this lovingly, you don't know what the hell you're talking about. Furthermore, you don't know what the hell you're doing either – and by the way – you never will. The only thing that changes is that by kid number 3 you will finally realize that your children are really going to be alright and with very little intervention on your part. Find them interesting, love them, give them responsibility, make them accountable, teach them compassion and get the hell out of the way. They will sometimes watch too much TV, they will sometimes not follow the rules, eat unhealthy food, be annoying, not listen, get on your nerves, run in public, yell in public, have tantrums, forget their homework, write on the walls, cover themselves head to toe in Vicks VapoRub, drink from the dog bowl, pee in a suitcase, never sleep through the night for 5 years, never eat what you make them for any meal AND drop Cheerios all over your life forever.

And guess what oh Great Mommy Swami – you will yell, cry, stomp, manipulate, punish, bribe, and turn on the TV. You'll be too tired for bedtime stories, not have play dates because you don't want to clean your house, say no when you should say yes – and vice versa. You'll yell, snipe, not give enough hugs, give too many passes, be unfair, "ruin" their lives, be hated, ignored, impatient and generally awful more often than you ever thought possible. This part IS all about you. Be firm consistently, be sorry when it's necessary, give love. Don't be afraid to say you were wrong – that happens in life sometimes – even to Mommy and Daddy. More to Daddy.

Guess what else?! The kids will probably cry on holidays or on birthdays after you've slaved for weeks planning every last second of that special event. One tiny thing will go wrong and they will devolve into a puddle of tears, snot, and unreasonableness. When it's all said and done you will ask, "Did you have fun?!" and they will say "NO!" You will do lots of things "for them" and you will expect a certain reaction that you will inevitably not receive. Don't let them be disrespectful but try not to tie up your self worth in their reactions to things. That's incredibly exhausting (and disappointing) for you and it puts a lot of power in those little hands. Our mommy world is crazy right now with competitive event planning, Pinterest insanity, and pressure galore to be perfect at everything all the time. It's not possible. Trying to be perfect ever much less all the time is not the point and quite honestly, those little people would rather just spend time with you. The happiest times are when you aren't doing anything special - together.

Oh dear, sweet, naive Me – I could go on infinitely but you should have the opportunity to find some of it out for yourself. Here's the thing: it's all worth it!

Good luck! I wish you much love, fortitude, and Xanax.

Love,

Future You

---

"I don't remember who said this, but there really are places in the heart you don't even know exist until you love a child."

**Anne Lamott**

---

# SO YOU THINK YOU CAN BE A PARENT?

F OR WHATEVER REASON, the universe thought it was a good idea to make us responsible for the wellbeing of other humans. In a hilarious nanny nanny boo-boo, the universe forgot to mention just how the hell we're supposed to do that.

Now some of you may have been fortunate enough to not be raised by insane people – maybe you actually came with instructions and/or had perfect parents. If that is the case would you please stand up and let us all see what that looks like and then can I tag your ear before we send you back out into the wild never to be seen again?

Some families are crazier than others' to be sure – but when it comes right down to it – no one really has any idea what they're doing. We just keep showing up for our kids everyday, trying to figure it out as we go.

And here we are at this moment without them getting ready to talk some serious shit about this "magnificent journey."

My mother names all of her cars "Betsy" – every single one of them – our first was a gigantic baby blue station wagon with one of those "way backs" that we could sit in because it was the 80's and no one cared about children back then - then another station wagon, two Honda Accords, and now a CRV that she's had for nearly 15 years. That last "Betsy" recently died but still sits in her drive way because the thought of getting rid of it makes her dissolve into a puddle of tears. She's so familiar with her cars that sometimes she even calls them "Betz," as in "She's a good girl, that Betz" – they all were...

My mom also anthropomorphized all our pets – "Don't pick-up the cat," she would say, "You're crashing his boundaries." Or "The dog and I have a fundamental personality conflict – we just can't seem to get on the same page." She was always very concerned about the health of her relationships with inanimate objects and animals. Mom doesn't have the same interest when it pertains to relationships with people. Living with bi-polar disorder at times means that her choices are unpredictable to say the least. Often they are made entirely from the perspective of anxiety reduction and conflict avoidance. Basically her motto is, "If someone upsets you, you should never speak to them again; don't tell them they've upset you, and if at all possible, you should move away." Nothing is worse than confrontation – nothing. She's still working on it.

I will say this: my mother is loving and kind hearted. She worked really hard to raise us and did her very best. Ultimately, in parenting, as in life, we start where we are and face the task with all our strengths, and limitations too. Being a mom or dad is not easy. I wanted to write and talk about it to let you all know that showing up is 99% of the battle. The rest is just details – some days, weeks, months are good and others are more challenging. My mom and I love each other a lot and guess what, I'm crazy too. But I think the thing I'm learning, that I didn't always know - is that no one is perfect. It's time to stop trying to appear as if we are. Let's embrace the beauty of imperfection because it's really all we have. I was raised by a crazy mother who loved me and did her best. It wasn't always enough yet here I am and I'm not an ax-murderer.

I recently had two dad friends of mine say, in two separate conversations, that they never felt like they were making the right decisions. They were afraid for their kids futures and worried that they were screwing-up.

In a true moment of clarity and peace , I leaned in to each of them and said, "Here's a secret: your kids are fine. The playing field is level in this instance. Not one parent on this earth knows what the hell they are doing. There isn't a secret handbook that some parents receive that others don't. No one knows. If you worry that you're screwing them up you're probably doing ok."

No matter how much I learn, read or experience as a parent – I always feel like I'm screwing it up there's comfort in knowing I'm not the only one.

---

"A life spent making mistakes is not only more honorable but more useful than a life spent doing nothing."

**George Bernard Shaw**

---

# BECOMING – 2006

THE TASK OF BECOMING is one in which no one ever develops expertise. Every day we embark on the path of becoming something more than we were yesterday. As a result it sometimes seems insane that we are allowed to bear and raise subsequent generations. Yet, somehow the complexity and enormity of the love we feel for our children suddenly makes knowing everything less important than learning what's important and letting everything else go.

There was a time when my ego would have prevented me from admitting that I did not possess the skill set to deal with certain situations. I would have plugged along, on my own, in the futile search for answers. But an amazing thing happens when you become a parent, your ego is suddenly smaller than your love for your child.

To this end you go out, admit defeat, and do everything you can to obtain the skills necessary to help your child become the remarkable person they are meant to be. There is no substitute for the sharing of experiences between people who hold the same goal. Everyone will ultimately find the path that works for them, and there are so many, but knowing that we are not alone in our journey is monumentally comforting.

This morning, armed with my new arsenal of knowledge obtained from last night's *Positive Discipline* class, three hours of sleep and the courage of my convictions I faced the coming day. As the sun shines after a storm or more likely, a lull before the onslaught, my usually uncooperative three year old dressed, ate, cleaned up and with a little coaxing and a game of tickle monster, put on her coat and went to school. Just before she left I said, "Thank you, sweet girl, for helping out this morning. You are an important part of our family and in a family everyone makes a contribution" to which she promptly replied, "a contribution to your PBS station" and walked out the door. Life is nothing if not full of unexpected little moments when you realize why you fight so hard to keep it together.

The travails of parenthood are matched by the joys. With every passing day the development of these people for whom you possess the ultimate responsibility is marked by new accomplishments, phrases, or the most hilariously uncoordinated dancing ever witnessed. The cooing and recognition of an infant whose existence is barely past being marked in weeks is now so deeply ingrained in my existence that I wonder what I used to do before. There are no words for this passage through space and time, no explanation for the happiness and helplessness, elation and exhaustion that come with the job except to say that it is not for the faint of heart or the weak of will. The extent of learning that one experiences through the eyes of our children cannot be matched in any school or by reading every book. To see yourself in the mirror of your own child is the ultimate lesson in humility.

---

"We live in a world in which we need to share responsibility. It's easy to say not my child, not my community, not my problem. Then there are those who see a need and respond. I consider those people my heroes."

**Mr. Rogers**

---

# BECOMING 2016

WHEN MY DAUGHTER was 3 years old, in 2006, I wrote a piece entitled "Becoming" about the "terrible threes." It was all about our challenges with setting expectations and moving through that difficult time when toddlers find their personalities and moms and dads have to realize that their sweet little babies are actually becoming people. Ten years later it's time for the next round of becoming.

I recently told my daughter that I had volunteered her for something in the community. Usually she just says ok and asks what she will be doing. But she's 12 now and she's becoming her own person. My girl has always been shy and reserved – hard for me to imagine being either of those things – but she has made a life of mostly going with the flow. So I was surprised when this time I told her she had been volunteered she spoke up.

"I don't mind helping mommy" Yes, she still calls me mommy "But I would really like it if you would ask me if I want to instead of just signing me up for things."

That hit me really hard. On the one hand I was a little annoyed that she would react to volunteering in this way because we are a family that places a lot of value on working in our community. However, on the other hand I was really proud to hear her speaking up for herself. I want to know that my daughter can be her own person and that she has a sense of herself enough to want to be asked to do things rather than just told. As the parent of a quiet child it's often difficult to know what is really going on inside her head. She is better adjusted and balanced than I could ever imagine being; but I haven't always felt confident that she would be able to voice her needs in the world. It's the fundamental difference between us – I have always been loud and emotional, and she is neither of those things. No one would ever wonder if I was ok with something or not. It's not always been so easy to tell with her.

Needless to say I was so glad to see her coming into herself in such a mature way. Insert deep parenting breath here, followed by the "Maybe everything will be ok after all" mantra. It's always been hard for me to envision that my kids would learn to do the things that everyone learns. I was sure that they wouldn't walk, talk, read or learn to cut their own food. Why? Who knows?! Probably because I'm neurotic as hell, and I'm always preparing for things that don't happen. I worry about them constantly. I try really hard not to let it come out on them because I want them to know I have expectations that they will be good, and do good, in the world. But in the back of my head I'm always waiting for what might happen.

A few weeks after this encounter I portrayed Dr. Carolyn Goodman, mother of slain civil rights activist Andrew Goodman in a play about the life of Dr. Martin Luther King Jr. In preparing for this role I read a lot about this family and took so much from Dr. Goodman's experience as a mother in the face of the horrific murder of her son and his fellow activists Mickey Schwerner and James Chaney. The death of a child is the greatest loss a person can face.

Goodman and her husband raised their children in a home filled with causes. They were always working to fix some injustice in their community and the world at large. Her son wanted to repair the world his entire, tragically short life. They had worked toward it as a family. And yet, when he came to her in mid-1964 and asked to go to Mississippi in response to the call to action from Dr. King, Dr. Goodman's first reaction was to say no. She knew it would be hard and dangerous and she was afraid for her son. She could never have imagined what he would really experience as a white, Jewish, civil rights worker in Mississippi in 1964 but what she did know is that it would be more difficult than anything he had ever done before.

After Andy's death she dedicated her life to ensuring that his sacrifice and the sacrifice of every man, woman and child killed or injured in the face of racism would not be in vain. When she was asked in later years if she had it to do over would she let him go? She responded "Yes" every time. She knew that helping people and fighting against injustice was the way her son wanted to, and was meant to, spend his life. It was not her job to hold him back from that destiny – it instead became her job to continue his legacy beyond his life.

My daughter standing up to me is clearly not the same as the enormous sacrifices that were made by the Goodmans, the Kings, the Schwerners, the Chaneys and the countless others who have given their lives to make our world better and safer for the future. However, every person who makes the decision to stand for something has a mother at home who is both proud and terrified. My daughter coming into her own in that way at that moment made me hopeful for a future when she wants things of the world and she is willing to speak out in hopes of making them happen.

We cannot always understand our children's motives, passions, or choices. That is not our job. Parents can only help children find their voice and empower them to use it in the world to speak for their own needs and to speak for the needs of those who cannot speak for themselves. It is our job as parents to prepare them to go out into the world and become whomever they are destined to be. I have been deeply inspired by Dr. Goodman through her books and writings. I hope that I am able to be the kind of mother to my children that she was to hers – instilling in them a voice, compassion, commitment and the willingness to stand-up for what they believe in.

# SEASONS

AHHH SUMMERTIME. From about late January – mid February I start to pray for Summer. The long warm days and short nights, lots of time to be outside planting, swimming, margaritas, beach vacations and relaxation. Much like childbirth and other traumatic experiences parents forget just what summer really is - an expensive, exhausting, exercise in futility. Now don't get me wrong, it's filled with fun and joy and family togetherness too but if the planning for summer doesn't begin far in advance then you end up with tiny ping pong balls bouncing aimlessly for 10 weeks from one bad idea to another.

Take for instance my son – the middle child, a 3.5 years old, who my husband affectionately refers to as #2 – because he's the second child not because he's a little shit – that's just a funny coincidence. He shares a room, in theory, with his baby brother. This means that the baby's crib is in the room but the baby still sleeps in the room with my husband and I – mostly because number 2 would never let the baby sleep otherwise. So the baby's crib has become a charming hiding place for all of big brother's concoctions or things he gets into that he doesn't want us to know about. Again - he's very, very stealthy. A career in military special ops would be a good fit for this skill.

My husband recently found a bucket filled with things that #2 had collected from around the house, a hand full of Q-tips, some nails, an unused "back-up" pregnancy test from the back of my bathroom. It's kind of like he's a witch with a cauldron because he's not comfortable just putting those things in the bucket he then has to fill it a quarter of the way with water and then hide it between the wall and the baby's crib, behind the curtains so no one can see it. I'm not sure what he's expecting will happen after he puts the water in but it makes for a lovely mess once we find it after a couple of days. We were happy to know that neither he, nor the bucket, are pregnant. That would be weird.

During the school year there is a reprieve from such behavior when they go to pre-school and have productive time with friends, and focus away from siblings and how "unfair" life is and how "mean" I am. I've tried desperately to arrange my house like school and to run on the school schedule when they are home – but the slightest deviation from the norm encounters great dissention among the ranks and leads to total anarchy. So we go out, if we can make it out of the house.

Sometimes I get halfway out of my neighborhood before I realize that I'm wearing my slippers or I've got the baby's breakfast all over the front of my shirt. At which point I have a very important decision to make, do we turn back and surely be waylaid another expanse of time or go out looking like a homeless person. The homeless person usually wins. The benefit of getting older and being a mom with multiple children is that one of two things is always true, either no one pays any attention to me or they are amazed I can function with three children under the age of 7 so the state of my personal appearance is a non-issue. Good for me on both counts.

I try to make up for it by looking extra nice when I go out sans children. That often blows up in my face too if my daughter wants to put my earrings on me, which she likes to put on backward, or the baby wants me to pick him up right before I leave the house – he inevitably has something on his hands - worse in his diaper - that makes its way onto my person. Fun!

Ahhh, the end of summer and fall's beginning. How magnificent the crisp air and the changing leaves, apple picking, decorations, and most of all summer is O.V.E.R. and the kids are back in school. All the parents understand - it's not that we don't love our children and love spending time with them but too much of any good thing is well – by August enough is enough.

Now of course I have never and will never tell my children to shut-up – just so no one gets the wrong impression. But oh how I'd love to. No, these days shut-up sounds like, "Ok, it's quiet time. Let's do a project." A project. It's so funny because we think this will be a great idea. Something they can do to keep them occupied, focused, and content. Well, about 35 seconds into the wonderfulness of the project it becomes a war zone. Screaming, throwing, grabbing.

"That's my paper!"

"No, I like that color!"

"Green is my favorite color!"

"Where's my glue? He stole my glue!"

"It's my glue, you use the other glue!"

"The other glue's not sticky enough. Give me!"

"NOOOO!!"

"Mommy he stabbed me with the safety scissors!"

"She wouldn't let me have the green!"

And I'm standing there thinking, "I wanted this. I am a f@*king lunatic. What the hell was I thinking? These people are going to become axe murderers. I have no impact, no control, and they are against me. AHHHHHHH!!!!" But I respond with, "There's enough paper for everyone and we can split the glue. Don't stab your sister with the scissors. It's not nice. If we're going to fight we can put the project away and spend time alone in our rooms." (Oh please dear God let them keep fighting so I can go to my room.)

Is it just me? Maybe I'm just a terrible mother but the chaos that is multiple children is nothing short of apocalyptic.

When I was a kid I was obsessed with Bill Cosby *Himself* the stand-up event where he talked about his life and life raising 5 children. Now I only have three children, one of which is the equivalent of 3 children by himself, but I often recall his talking about the lovely woman who he rode on a plane with and her son Jeffrey. Maybe you remember, the woman got on the plane beautiful and pulled together and exited the flight looking like a haggard troll. She began sweetly saying, "Jeffrey come here," "No Jeffrey" and after 4 hours or so on the flight she was reduced to a tight lipped, whisper yelling, shell of her former self "Jeffrey, Jeffrey, Jeffrey". That is how I feel at the end of some days. I wake with hope and excitement for the wonderful day that we will have together. Then they fight, yell, scream, cry, destroy the order of the house, whine, redeem themselves for awhile and play nicely together which lulls me into a false sense of security and just when I've recovered from them and feel that our wonderful day can begin, "Nooooooo!!!!! I hate you!" "Mommy he said a bad word." "She was mean to me!"

Some days I can't even make it out of the house. It's probably better that way, so as to spare the world the insanity.

# GOING ON A TRIP

GETTING A FAMILY READY to go on a trip is a little like going to war, or so I imagine. There are strategies, plans to be formulated and executed. You have to decide what supplies are essential and what is superfluous and will only, in the end, hold you back. Being a mom is a lot like being a general. It is essential to remain calm in the face of what's ahead. I'm still not good at that. There is no doubt that there will be setbacks and sacrifices along the way. The thought must always be for the collective, never the individual. In the end if most of your men make it to where they are supposed to be in relatively good condition, then you did your job and the mission was a success.

Tomorrow we fly to Atlanta for a wedding and my house looks as if it has been hit by a bomb. We have scheduled two open houses while we're out of town. What were we thinking?!? The baby refuses to go to sleep because he's teething. The two big kids didn't go to bed until almost 9 pm and not for lack of trying on my part for nearly an hour and a half. The excitement in our house is radiating and I need a drink!

Every time we plan a trip I am equally excited and angry at myself for thinking it was a good idea. I started packing a week ago and yet there are still things I'm certain I've forgotten. I've made list after list and still feel like I might leave my own arms and legs behind. Then I'd surely get to take a nap, right?! After a week of trying to get the house in order for the showings that will certainly happen - eventually - and the open houses that are on the books - I've gotten two bathrooms cleaned. HOORAY! I suck.

My day begins at 5:30 and usually ends somewhere between 10 p.m. and midnight. I never have time for lunch and it's almost 10 right now and I haven't eaten dinner. Nothing ever feels finished. I truly feel like a chicken with its head cut off. I am 'Mike, the headless chicken' darting about frantically and just when I think maybe I've gotten somewhere comes the realization that I no longer have a head and therefore don't know here from there - somewhere is anywhere.

Eventually I take a breath and look over at the stubborn, little, round headed baby sitting on the floor next to me with an enormous binkie in his mouth playing with my cell phone. He is panting excitedly as he turns the phone over and over in his little hands. Why don't they ever get that much joy out of their own toys?

He will sleep – one day.

We're going to have fun and I've got to let go. Whatever we forget will not be missed. Someone will buy our house and if not then I will just give it away. After all, it's only a house.

# WHO'S REALLY IN CHARGE HERE?

OUR CHILDREN HAVE A WAY of making us know very early on that we are in fact not in control of any part of this process. When I was young...I was a singer and actor. I wanted more – I wanted to be a mom. I got married and began my family. I was done with the stage. It was time to dedicate my life to the service of others – "I will sing to my kids," I said. Until my first child – my daughter – was two years old – I sang to her day and night. I read stories with funny voices and cried over how meaningful every moment of this all was. It was magic. Then one day she uttered those famous words, "Mommy stop singing. You're hurting my ears." It didn't stop there because soon she was asking me to read to her in my "regular voice." She was really bumming me out.

This was the beginning of the end. I started realizing that I am not in control. Not in any real sense. They are going to like what they like, do what they do, and nothing is ever going to be picture perfect as it was in my dreams of being a parent before reality took hold. At least not unless I'm cool with Stepford children - which I think would be super creepy.

I had these great visions of beautiful, meaningful heart to hearts with my children before they were born. Just before my daughter's seventh birthday I decided it was time to take her to

New York City. It had been my favorite place on Earth since I first visited when I was 11. We left early on the morning of her birthday, and drove six hours up 95 from Richmond to my friend's house in Cliffside Park, New Jersey. It was just across the Hudson River from the city. We would save a few dollars by sleeping at her place, and then we could take the ferry into the city. I made dinner reservations, booked front row orchestra seats to the new Broadway production of *Mary Poppins*, and planned all of the 'must see' sites I could possibly fit in a quick two-day trip.

We arrived and made our way into the City without delay. Straight away she got a hot dog from a street vendor – and because I was vegan this was the beginning of her asserting her independence. We had tea at the Plaza, took a Pedi-cab ride through Central Park, went to the American Girls store, FAO Schwartz and rode the ferris wheel in ToysRus. That night we met another friend of mine and had dinner at a tiny but incredibly delicious Italian restaurant in the Theatre District. Here my daughter discovered her love of fried calamari – and then the three of us headed to the theatre! What a magical day.

We got back late that night and snuggled up, basking in the glow of our incredible day. The next morning, we got up early and headed back into the City. It was a cloudy day. She was tired but game for a little more fun. We went to the top of the Empire State Building but couldn't see a thing through the heavy clouds. It was a really yucky day and we were both tired, so instead of another busy day, we decided to take it easy.

We continued to walk through the streets taking in everything so vastly different from our daily lives. I began what I imagined to be a great mother-daughter heart-to-heart. A talk that would open the floodgates to my sweet girl's deepest thoughts and feelings.

"You know honey, this is Mommy's favorite place to visit. I love this city so much and I am so happy to share it with you. The city represents all of the stuff I love the most – theatre, different cultures, art, music. Do you like it here?"

"Yes." she replied smiling up at me.

"Is there something that you love so much like that? Something that makes you feel happy and excited?" I asked her enthusiastically.

"Oh yes, mommy!" she replied with equal enthusiasm.

Here we go! I thought to myself. This is the moment when I learn something about my little girl. The moment when we grow closer and our relationship will be deepened forever.

"What is it honey?" Thinking she would tell me that she loved the theatre, art, music, and multi-culturalism as much as any newly seven-year-old person was able. Hoping she would share my passion for the things that had taken my entire 32 years on Earth to develop a love and understanding of. She was about to reveal to me her genius, emotional maturity, and then we would move to a new plane of existence together. I waited with anticipation for her answer.

With the deepest passion in her voice, she looked up at me and replied, "I really like telling people what to do."

This was not the answer I was expecting, although I was impressed by her commitment and self-knowledge.

"Well there are a lot of areas of life where that will come in very handy." I replied. "So, this was such a fun trip, do you think you would like to come back here with mommy sometime soon?"

"No, I don't think so." She said with a nonchalance that I'm certain wasn't meant to break my heart but it did a little. She had indeed revealed something very important to me, my children are not an extension of me. They don't have to and clearly won't like all of the things that excite me. It's hard to remember that sometimes. Fortunately they find regular opportunities to remind me.

---

"I was a wonderful parent, before I had children."

**Adele Faber**

---

# I HATE WIND

ONE NIGHT WHEN HE WAS 4, #2 woke-up in the middle of the night. He was too old to be sleeping with us. That, of course, was when I had standards, now I wake up with them sleeping on top of me and I'm unphased.

I got up and led him whimpering back to his room the whole time.

"You have to sleep in your bed buddy."

"NO!" he cried, which of course was killing me.

I stroked his hair and said, "You are a big boy and you have to sleep in your big boy bed."

He started to do that thing where they yell/cry. His eyes were closed, there were no tears, just absolute misery.

"I DON'T WANT TO GROW UP. I WANT TO STAY 3. I DON'T WANT TO BE 4. I'M GOING TO STOP EATING SO I CAN STAY SMALL."

"Oh," I respond.

"I HATE THIS!"

"I'm sorry you're unhappy." I say.

"I HATE MY BED. I HATE MY FRIENDS. I HATE SCHOOL."

It was summer. He wasn't even in school.

"AND I HATE WIND, AND I HATE SNOW. I NEVER WANT TO PLAY OUTSIDE IN THE SNOW AGAIN!"

"I thought you liked the snow." I said trying to – I don't know what the hell I was trying to do.

"NO – I HATE IT! I WANT TO STAY INSIDE WITH MOMMY."

"Oh – I really like playing outside in the snow." Again, I should have just kept my mouth shut but I didn't because I'm an idiot.

"YOU CAN'T LEAVE ME INSIDE BY MYSELLLLLLFFFFF!"

His eyes were closed and he was lying on his pillow throughout this entire interaction. There was nothing I could say to make it better. I should have just kept my mouth shut but I am hopeful and filled with hubris. I don't even remember what happened next – I assume he fell asleep. He did play outside in the snow again and I did not have to leave him inside by himself.

When they were little I felt like every time they cried, every pain was going to scar them for life. I worried all the time that I would – or the world would – destroy them. Childhood and adolescence had been so difficult for me. I was so sensitive, so easily hurt, as a young person that I wanted to protect my babies from that kind of pain. I obviously still want to protect them as much as possible but the thing it took me more time to realize about myself was that I was really strong and the pain didn't break me. The best thing I could do for them was to reasonably and responsibly let them stumble through life feeling the stings of failure and disappointment as much as the joy of success.

They are unpredictable and yet so much stronger than we give them credit for. They begin as little guinea pigs and we hope to know enough to not destroy them but in the end, parents are only born when they have children. We cannot possibly know what or how until faced with the magnificent challenge. We figure it all out with them. Whether you are wealthy or not; older or younger; highly educated or from the school of hard knocks, you don't know what the hell parenting means for you until you are in the middle of it.

---

"We could never learn to be brave and patient, if there were only joy in the world."

**Helen Keller**

---

# 'TIL THERE WAS YOU

---

"When my kids become wild and unruly, I use a nice safe playpen. When they're finished, I climb out."

**– Erma Bombeck**

---

For all of the crazy making and whining on my part, life didn't make sense to me until I was a wife and mother. In my best efforts to psychoanalyze myself I can only figure that my purpose is to make sense of the family dynamic. Maybe that's because I am a child of multiple divorces and I needed to make sense of it in real time with my actual life as America's Test Kitchen for family wellness. Regardless, I was never so grounded or filled with purpose until I became a wife and mother. I know, not a very feminist thing to say and not the way I would recommend finding your way in the world but it has worked for me. Maybe a gap year in Europe could have also been effective butI guess we'll never know.

Creating a family is a daily endeavor. You don't just do it and it's done. You do it every day and you have to be better than you ever thought you could be. Better at what? Just better. More patient (the most significant of my flaws is impatience), smarter, more organized (pretty terrible at this), nicer (also not a strength). You have to know what you think and what you believe when you are a parent. You have to be able to tell them about the world in a way that makes sense to them..

My daughter told us once at the dinner table that a person isn't dead until they go to Hell.

"Really?" I said – thinking to myself 'this ought to be interesting'.

"Yes."

"Well honey, we don't really believe in Hell. Who told you about Hell?"

"Molly"

"In your class?"

"Uh-huh"

"And she told you that a person isn't dead until they go to Hell?"

"Yep"

"What else did she say?"

"Nothing"

"Where is Hell?"

"Under the ground"

"Is it a good place or a bad place?"

"Bad – only bad people go to hell"

"Where do good people go?"

"Heaven"

"Where is heaven?"

"In the sky"

"I see"

"What happens there?"

"I don't know."

I've always been a very gray area kind of person. I hate taking a multiple choice type test because even with multiple choices, they're always so definite. Would you do this or this? "Well it depends," I find myself saying. I took a Myers Briggs personality test at work once and almost burst into flames. It was incredibly stressful. When I got the results I found that I am the master of the universe. I wish someone had told me that sooner – I would have made the most of it.

In explaining the world to a child I find myself getting very complicated. Children see the world in absolutes, black and white. This happens here and that happens there and there are good people and bad people and that's that. So heaven and hell works really well for children – I've never figured out how adults can hang onto the notion but that's another conversation for a less politically correct day.

Motherhood is NEVER how we think it will be...for better AND worse.

My primary goal in life was to have a family. Old fashioned maybe, but still the truth. When I made the decision to give up being a singer and actor, it was for many reasons but in the end I always said that I would sing to my children and that would fulfill me. That is true and it does.

In the beginning of my motherhood journey it really was enough to sing to them, for awhile. TThat day when my daughter was two and I was singing along with the radio in the car and she piped up from the back seat "Stop singing Mommy! You're hurting my ears," began awakening me to a hard truth. The first time she said this I laughed because it was funny but that was also a glimmer into the reality that I could not look to my family to fulfill all the parts of me. They wouldn't want to listen to me every time I needed to belt out a song. I believe I have mentioned already: this isn't about us parents.

Bubbe loved that I could sing - so much so that she forced me to do so at every holiday, party, and gathering - whether others wanted me to or not. Rarely did she ask me to sing when she and I were alone. It's interesting to think that my talent was somehow a validation of her to others. I'm honored that she thought so highly of me but it was a little too much sometimes.

I guess in the end there is comfort in the fact that they still request that I sing to them often and now we all sing together. These days I'm asking them to serenade me. They love to listen to my recordings but they still are not concerned in the least by asking me to be quiet when they've had enough. Maybe there isn't such a thing as balance and I shouldn't be so analytical - but this seems close enough to me.

Besides, one day they'll be in therapy for something for which I will almost certainly receive the blame. If it's that I sang too much, things could be worse...

# WHY WOULD YOU PEE IN THAT?

O NE NIGHT AFTER I had peacefully put my daughter to bed and not so peacefully put my older son (3 years old) to bed 7 or 8 times I was finally sitting down to eat a meal at around 8:30 pm. I hear my son calling me from the top of the stairs. Flustered and a little bit annoyed I walk to find him standing up there with no pants or pullup on. Naked from the waste down. "What are you doing buddy?" I asked.. "Why are you naked?"

He then points to the baby's bathtub which is sitting outside the bathroom on the floor. He begins to mutter under his breath but I can't understand what he's saying. I go up the stairs to find the bathtub with a small yellow puddle in it. "Did you pee pee in the bathtub?" He smiles and nods his head at me. "We don't do that honey. What made you want to do that?" He answered, "I just wanted to" and walked back to his room and got into bed still naked from the waste down. This is what I call boy logic.

Needless to say, I cleaned out the baby's bathtub, put a pull-up on the boy, and got him down to sleep. What is so unbelievable to me is that the child has no interest in potty training at all. He refuses to go in any kind of potty on a regular basis. Yet, he has no trouble disrobing at absolutely the wrong time and urinating in the place where his baby brother is bathed.

My mother dramatically insists that it's a sort of alpha male marking of territory. I, however, do not believe it to be that well thought out. I simply think he found himself at the top of the stairs, he saw the bathtub, and decided he'd like to pee on it. End of story. In my journey through motherhood I am working to understand the motivations of my children's behaviors. This example however, proves that any real attempt to do so is futile because the behavior is completely unpredictable. I can only take a deep breath and try not to lose my mind.

-------

"Having children is like having a bowling alley installed in your brain."

**Martin Mull**

-------

# BOY LOGIC...

I HAVE REALIZED SINCE becoming a parent of little boys that household items, food, cleaning products, body care, etc. are in fact meant for many more exciting purposes than I could have ever imagined - at least to three year old little boys!

Every #2 event (and yes, they are events) begins the same way - with the cliché of the mother realizing that the house is far too quiet. Followed by a search throughout the house calling, "#2! Where are you?" To no avail, I might add because little boys have selective hearing - especially when they're hiding from you doing something they know you're not going to like! Virtually every time, when I finally locate him, he greets me with the proudest smile, as if to say: "Look Mommy at what a wonderful and creative boy I am!" I respond with the requisite, "How could you have possibly done all this in so little time?!?!" Time to clean up another mess...

The three year old year was one I would never want to trade and yet I am hoping - now that he's recently turned 4 - that the fascination with such experimentation will take a more scaled down approach. It all started one day when I found him in the, closet standing, naked, inside my husband's empty laundry basket doing a little dance.

"What are you doing in there buddy?" I innocently asked.

"I'm skating," he smiled. "With lotion," he stated deviously.

He had squirted an entire bottle of lotion into the bottom of the basket which created a virtual skating rink for his little feet to slip and slide in to his heart's content. That was the beginning but it took a few more times for me to finally catch on.

It is important to note that just prior to #2 turning three, his baby brother was born. The baby never, and I mean NEVER slept, making mommy a little nutty and a lot fruity. Therefore, my peripheral vision and hearing were impacted to some degree leaving open a large window for #2 to experiment a bit more freely than he might have otherwise.

The next was the time I found him behind the curtains in my bedroom with a paint brush and a tube of the baby's Vaseline. "Look Mommy, I'm painting your wall!" Awesome.

There was a lull in said behavior as I began to catch on and confiscated nearly everything in the house ensuring a #2 proof location. For a while there was nothing that he could get into. Until one night, our oldest had a cold and she asked for some Vicks VapoRub. I obliged and while I religiously remember to put such things back up on the highest shelf that night - I did not. I left it in her room on her dresser after #2 had gone to bed.

The next morning I walked out of my bedroom to be met by a naked boy covered from hair to toes in...wait for it...Vicks VapoRub. He smiled proudly up at me stating "Look Mommy, I'm all shiny!"

After toweling, bathing, and toweling again he still had a film and repeated over and over again "I'm cold Mommy," to which I replied "I'm sure you are buddy. You'll just have to wait for it to wear off."

Around Halloween things took a more dramatic turn. One day I was in the family room with #2 and the baby sitting on the floor – the girl was in school. Please note that if she were ever around during any of these escapades they surely would not have happened. We don't call her The Enforcer for nothing. #2 announces that he needs to go upstairs to get something and he will be right back. Well after a very short amount of time I call to him - I'm catching on at this point and I wasn't allowing him to wander far for long. I called again and he answers from the kitchen "I'm in the kitchen just cleaning up a little mess."

I remained seated and for a split-second thinking to myself "Isn't that nice!" Lack of sleep was really getting to me by then. I quickly snapped out of it, got up, and went into the kitchen. It took me a second to realize what I stepped in but when it dawned on me that I was standing in a pile of flour as deep as my foot I was shocked. I looked up to find flour - an entire brand new bag of flour - creating a five-foot trail from the pantry, where it had previously lived, to the foot of the staircase. At the bottom of the staircase was the boy standing in the giant pile of flour that he had dumped out when he'd reached his destination. I suppose I should have been thankful that he didn't try to take it upstairs. The most shocking thing is that I had been sitting less than 10 feet away and I never heard a thing. The kid is stealthy!

He stood in the pile of flour that covered his feet like they were buried in sand at the beach. In his hand he held a little toy broom and he was determined to sweep up all the flour with this tiny little thing. Next to him was the head of Dora the Explorer, the empty bag of flour, an ice cream scoop, and one yellow rubber kitchen glove. It looked like the scene of a very strange crime. He looked at my astonished, speechless face and smiled nonchalantly, as if this were something he did all the time - then he went back to sweeping.

I'm always fairly certain during these events that he knows what he's doing is not a good choice and yet the pride with which he attacks these undertakings tells me otherwise. Further, he is always just as happy as can be to clean up after them. I take that back, he will clean up until he's done cleaning whether the work is done or not. I honestly don't remember what happened next except that I took pictures.

Within the same month, he was having a particularly good day as he had recently tackled potty training. He was very proud of this newfound freedom. On this day, I had picked him up from school and brought him home for lunch. I made lunch while he played. He announced that he was going to the bathroom and could I please turn on the light. As a parent those are the moments that make the chaos worthwhile. It was a lovely peaceful afternoon and all was right with the world.

Famous last words...

As I finished preparing lunch for him and the baby I reveled in the sound of #2 washing his hands, singing, and playing in the sink - which I saw no problem with since I had always let his sister do it. A couple of minutes passed and I went to get him to come have lunch. I walked into the bathroom to find him playing sweetly. The sink was filled with bubbles and he had toys on the counter. I pulled out the stopper and put my hands into the bubbles to get the toys out. Since there were bubbles I couldn't see THE ENTIRE ROLL OF TOILET PAPER he had shredded into the sink full of soap and water.

I pulled out a handful and looked at him. Again, he had the proudest smile on his face. "Look Mommy I made goop!!" And once again, before I did anything I took pictures.

Then he helped me pull the crud out of the drain and deposit all of it in the trash. I explained that it was not ok to use the toilet paper to make 'goop'. He didn't understand how anything that great could be bad. But he never did it again so I assume I got through...

All these years later he continues to astonish us every day with his wit, curiosity, and spirit. If I don't end up in a mental hospital there will always be an abundance of stories to fill our days. It's never boring, that's for sure.

---

"To everything there is a season and a time to every purpose under heaven."

**Ecclesiastes Chapter 3 Verse 1**

---

# MORE BOY LOGIC

I REALLY DON'T KNOW how to express the level of bewilderment I possess for what goes on in my 3 year old boy's head. He's the most joyful, exuberant, emotional little thing. Recently, we had a stray dog find its way into our yard. It was one of those stifling late summer days here in Richmond when it feels like the air forgot how to move, and you might suffocate the second you walk outside. It was the last week of summer and the energy of change was palpable in the stagnant air. Everyone in the house was electrified and so when the poor old black mutt my daughter affectionately named 'Rosebud' found her way into our yard you can imagine the excitement. The whole ordeal lasted less than an hour but it left a lasting impression.

Since we no longer have a fence spanning to whole of our backyard I decided to hold the dog on the screened porch and call the county animal control to find the dog's owner. She had a rabies tag but no name tag or license. She was sweet and panting heavily so I felt comfortable letting the kids around her. You just have a feeling about these things and I knew she would be gentle and she was. I got her a bowl of water because she was panting so much and it was so hot outside. It took her a few minutes to drink from the bowl but she finally did. The kids were so interested in everything this poor dog was doing. In the meantime, I called the county and found the dog's owner who happened to live on our street even though I'd never seen her. I called the owner and left a message stating that I would wait for a call because I didn't want to release the dog to possibly get hit by a car.

While I waited to hear back, the children - consisting of my 3 year old son and his friend, my almost 6 year old daughter and her friend, and my 4 month old son - all very enthusiastically played with the dog. My daughter desperately wanted to keep her and I had to explain why we couldn't but that when the little ones got a little older we too could get a dog. That was an undertaking for which I was definitely not ready! She accepted that answer reluctantly and enjoyed playing with 'Rosebud'.

The 3-year-old however, was vibrating with excitement. He danced and yelled and then he did something completely unexpected. Something that leaves me speechless and giggling to this day. He walked over to the water bowl that the dog had been drinking from and crouched down looking intently at it. Then he stood up, said "Mmm doggie water", put his finger in the bowl and sucked the water off as if it were brownie batter!

I watched and said nothing. Honestly, I didn't really know what to say. I don't ever remember being that happy to be alive, to figure out how the world works. I admire it - even if it often drives me nuts - or in this case turns my stomach. He is just happy to be alive. I've always called him my 'joyful boy' because he just smiles and loudly enjoys life. He has huge, bright eyes and when he was a little baby his eyes would get so big and he wouldn't blink. It was sometimes off putting to have this baby staring like that but really it just seemed like he was afraid that if he blinked he would miss something.

I don't want him or his sister and brother to miss a single thing. I want them all to have the magical childhoods they deserve.

They inspire me to be better, they enlighten me to those things which are truly important in this world, and they frustrate me to no end. They never let me forget that their lives are not about me - as much as I have the tendency to make everything about me. I still struggle to find the balance between attentive mother and mommy martyr; and some days are better than others. I guess I'll keep working at it and I'll have 'boy logic' to keep me entertained and exasperated.

---

"Without deviations from the norm progress is not possible."

**Frank Zappa**

---

# LESSONS LEARNED IN A MOVIE THEATER PARKING LOT

O URS IS A COMPLICATED TIME. Raising children in an echo chamber of opinions, social media hype, sound bites and hysteria for its own sake has the potential to make us want to go off grid. I consider this option at least once a week. Increasingly, the lesson our children learn is that society rewards the person with the loudest and most outrageous point of view. Which can make it even more challenging to raise thoughtful, engaged, respectful humans.

I was once a loud, opinionated young person filled with passionate ideas. I regularly judged others who I deemed "stupid" because they didn't share my point of view. I remain opinionated, passionate and idealistic. However, time and experience have taught me the value of being gentler in the expression of my thoughts and in the practice of my principles. While self-righteousness can feel good in the moment, it is generally unsuccessful when attempting to get people to think of things in a different way. Ultimately, that's the charge – not being the loudest voice but being the most effective in opening minds. This work is more nuanced, often less exciting in the moment, and a lot harder to learn.

It's interesting how these lessons present themselves – often very uncomfortably – and we can look back at those moments as being formative. I remember the day I learned that talking to people was more effective than yelling, being accusatory, or vilifying what I perceived as willful ignorance. It was a powerful day.

In the summer of 2008 the film *Tropic Thunder* was released. You may, or may not, remember that this film was controversial for the use of the "R-word". I was working for the Department of Mental Health Support Services and we got a call from a local advocacy organization that the film's language flew in the face of the work we did every day. We were asked to come out for a "protest rally" and to recruit others who might be interested. Advocates across the state had been working for several years to change the official diagnosis for those we served from mental retardation to intellectual disability. The consensus was that "retardation" had become derogatory and was no longer an innocuous medical diagnosis. The use of this word in the film was upsetting and it also felt like an opportunity to educate the public on these changes.

In our roles as Service Coordinators we worked to support those with intellectual disabilities to be as independent as possible and to put appropriate supports in place where needed. We helped in obtaining and maintaining social services, Medicaid, education, jobs, transportation, medical and dental care, clothing, camps, holiday meals, social opportunities, advocacy, counseling, and more. My colleagues and I were deeply committed to building a world in which the needs of these individuals were met and most importantly that they were treated with dignity and respect within our community. So when I was asked to take part in this protest, I said of course – but I had no idea what to expect or how to approach this endeavor.

In the few years leading up to that day I had become a wife and mother, worked in the House of Delegates; gone back to school; canvassed for political campaigns and actively got involved in my community. I worked the polls for causes which were important to me, and engaged in passionate discourses on local politics, social issues with vitriol and judgement. Yet, there weren't a lot of opportunities for protest rallies in Chesterfield County.

Yet with all that experience standing up for what I believe in – I didn't feel comfortable representing myself, my profession, the people I served, or my agency as part of an angry mob yelling about a movie. But the cause was so important to me that I felt the weight of this important task: getting people to hear what I had to say. Somehow I knew that publicly shaming folks on their way to the movies, in the middle of the day on a Tuesday, would not be the right approach. This was about more than being right, it was about people's lives and dignity.

When I arrived there weren't many protesters and we were spread throughout a very large parking lot leading to the biggest movie theater in the county at the time. I was immediately relieved not to see the angry mob I had feared. Each participant was handed a stack of flyers with information about the lack of services and resources for people with intellectual disabilities and sent on our way. I didn't know the best way to approach this task. My passion for the cause outweighing my anxiety, I just started walking up to people. It went something like this:

"Are you on your way to see *Tropic Thunder* by chance?"

If they said yes I would ask for a moment of their time and continue.

"Hi, my name is Erin and I work with individuals with intellectual disabilities living in Chesterfield County. We work every day to support the needs of an incredibly diverse group of people and their families. In the film *Tropic Thunder*, the "R-Word" is used to derogatorily refer to a person with disabilities."

The first responses I got were fairly innocuous. Some people told me they had heard about it and they didn't use the word, told me to have a nice day and politely brushed me off. I wasn't deterred. I just thanked them, handed the flyer and went about my business. Then there was the man. He got out of a pick-up and was smoking a cigarette. He wore an old flannel shirt over a dirty t-shirt and jeans with work boots, medium length hair covered in an old baseball cap. I debated whether or not to approach him because he didn't look very friendly but I had come to do a job so I steeled myself and made my way over. My initial assessment was pretty spot on. He was not particularly friendly nor did he want to talk to me about my hippie agenda.

"Oh good lord!" he replied after I gave him my initial spiel. "The word police are here. I'm not interested."

I was shaking at this moment but I quickly considered my options.

1. I can let this man go about his day and leave well enough alone. He's not going to listen to me.

2. I can let him get the better of me and engage in a yelling match in the parking lot.

3. I can carefully share with him my perspective however shaky or sappy it may feel. I can walk the walk.

I decided on the third option. It's pretty terrifying to stand in front of someone who didn't expect to be talking to you about something they think is a giant waste of time, when all they want is popcorn and a cherry coke. Growth is hard and usually uncomfortable. I took a deep breath.

"Sir, I'm not asking you to not go see the movie. I'm not even asking you not to laugh. All I'm asking you to do is think about the impact of that word. I work with folks with intellectual disabilities every day and they are people just like you and me working hard and doing their best to have the best life possible. That word was established to describe a diagnosis but now it has become something that is used to tell them that they are worthless and it's hurtful."

"Uh-huh," he said still appearing disinterested, but not walking away and not yelling at me so I decided to finish saying my piece.

"All I'm asking is for you to think about it while you're watching the movie and maybe also in your life. I just want you to know that that word has the power to hurt people and you have the power to not. Thank you so much for your time and I hope you enjoy the movie."

He continued not making eye contact but mumbled, "Yeah, I'll think about it" as he walked away. Maybe he would, maybe he wouldn't, in that moment it didn't really matter.

I had spent my entire young life being terrified of confrontation. I was one of those people who was so afraid of facing off with someone that I would immediately begin yelling and crying. Maybe you can relate? Maybe I'm a super weirdo – don't worry I'm very used to that. Either way this was one of the most successful confrontations of my life to that point. I didn't yell or insult him. I wasn't self-righteous or condescending. Something came over me and I became calm and reasonable. I actually said those words in that moment. I'll never forget it as long as I live because I couldn't believe my brain was so cooperative. I think I may even have done the touchdown dance.

I talked to a lot of people that day and received many varied responses. Some people thanked me, others completely ignored me but what I learned in front of that movie theater in the middle of the suburbs is that confrontation is more about how I choose to react than it is about what I am met with.

That day felt like a huge success to me because I was able to have some real conversations with people. Did anyone have a magnificent epiphany in that parking lot? If they did I was not aware of it but no one yelled or insulted anyone. It's really difficult to scream at someone who is humble and sincere. It can be terrifying to make yourself vulnerable like that which is why, I imagine, many people approach conflict with aggression. They're afraid too and they figure if they yell really loud no one will be willing to push back and then it will be over. (Or you might just find them with their hands over their over ears, rocking in the fetal position).

This is what I try to impart to my children when preparing them for the world. Fighting indifference with anger, or anger with judgement will not produce the outcomes we desire. Asking a person to consider your perspective while also being open to understanding theirs' is the only way to find common ground. It has to be about personal accountability. We cannot wait for people to be ready to hear what we have to say, instead we have to say it in a way in which they feel compelled to listen. Our words have enormous power – the power to hurt, the power to heal, the power to develop understanding, and the power to break it down entirely. There's no guarantee you will change anybody's mind but you might just change how you see yourself and your ability to stand up for the things you value.

---

"We meet aliens everyday who have something to give us. They come in the form of people with different opinions."

**William Shatner**

---

# MOTHER'S DAY: THE REJECTING PERFECT EDITION

KIDS ARE WEIRD AND parenthood is hard. There are no two ways about it. These people are loud. They talk through all of the tv shows and movies I want to watch. They expect meals everyday. They shit up my stuff. They think their little, beautiful faces, sweet voices, adorable talking, and general amazingness is enough to make it ok that they eat all of the things I buy for myself – and they are right.

I don't care about Mother's Day but I take advantage of it. Why? Because these little f@*kers need to learn to appreciate things. On Mother's Day they make me breakfast and coffee and deliver cards to me that they've made by hand. They look at me for a few seconds because their father has told them they have to and then they leave. They kiss me. They hug me. They thank me. They wish me a Happy Mother's Day. It all seems perfectly sincere and adorable but I know better than to believe them. I know the truth.

They don't like anything I enjoy. If I want to go to a play – they want to go to the movies. If I want to go to a festival they want to stay home, and not go to a festival. They don't like big groups of people, or fun things, or things I enjoy, or happiness – unless it includes fighting during things I like, eating my food, or crying because they don't want to do the things I like. Have I mentioned they are also weird? I can't say I'm surprised because I gave birth to them but yeah – they're super weird.

Today, my middle child came into the kitchen with a giant balloon that he wanted to fill with water. I told him that he needed to go to the bathroom sink with it. Next thing I know I walk in to the bathroom and he's in the tub, with his bathing suit on and the balloon is so huge and filled with water that he can't event lift the thing. I cleaned the bathroom around his mishegas, ignored the balloon situation except to ask him not to over flow the bathtub, and left. I have no idea what happened to that balloon. All I know is that it didn't explode inside the house. For all I know it's still sitting in the bathtub. When I left the bathroom I never thought about the balloon again – until right now.

Long ago I gave up even trying to be a perfect mom. I love them, feed them, clothe them, bathe them, buy stuff for them within reason, give them time with friends, celebrate their accomplishments, hug and kiss them, stick to bed time, don't beat them, make them eat broccoli on occasion, and expect them to treat people and things with respect. That's all I got.

They each have a bin in which to put their shoes when they come in the house. The bins are all empty but the area around the bins is littered with shoes. It's like a tiny collection of shoes that they've laid at the altar of "the bin." The shoes are little offerings. I hope it's religious because if not it's just assholeness.

I have tried a handful of times to create specialty, themed baked goods for their birthdays. The first time I baked a beautiful cake and made pink icing for my daughter's birthday. The cake split down the middle and my brother-in-law pointed out that the cake split down the middle with pink icing made it look like a vagina. I considered that quite a success. So much so, that I have done it a few more times creating cakes with faces that looked like they were in the middle of an aneurysm, racetracks that appeared to be in the aftermath of an earthquake, and other lopsided, tortured creations. It's certain that I will be opening a bakery very soon.

They wear what they want – most of the time it doesn't match. Other than the Jewish holidays I don't care what they wear. If their little behinds are covered and the clothes mostly fit I'm good. The little one doesn't like to change his clothes before he goes to sleep at night, nor does he like to have sheets or blankets on his bed. He likes only junk food and fruit. I fear the future of a child who never takes no for an answer, can charm his way out of (or in to) any situation and lives like a homeless person sleeping in his clothes on a blank mattress eating only goldfish and plums. It makes me completely nuts. After the fourth night in a row of re-making his bed I just say screw it and let him follow his bliss.

The girl told me yesterday that she prefers dogs to people and plans to live alone in a big house, as a very successful artist and have many dogs, next door to me and her dad, when she grows up. I love that she loves us so much but I did inform her that she can house sit because when she and her brothers, grow-up we plan to travel all the time. She said that was fine and made a plan for how she would care for our house. She was born 90 and is far more mature and well adjusted than I am. There was nothing weird, at all, about this conversation or the fact that my kid looks forward to being a dog-lady when she grows up and living next door to her parents. It's perfectly normal.

Tonight my husband and I tried to watch a movie with the kids. The little one watched Minecraft videos on YouTube for half the movie, the big one jumped on a mini-trampoline the entire time, and the middle one just wandered around the room and occasionally fell on the floor and tried to do the worm. We just kept turning up the volume.

In the rest of my life I am a control freak. I really tried to continue that pattern at home but they broke me. Long ago, they broke me. I didn't have a lot of sanity to begin with, and I wanted to keep the little bit I did have. I had high hopes that I would be able to be one of those always gorgeous, calm, organized, crafty, smiling, mommy's. Hope is for the weak and the stupid. So I stopped trying to make every moment a f@*king greeting card and just tried to get through it without lighting my own head on fire.

I love these people. I keep showing up everyday. We are all still alive and I'm only slightly medicated – so...success. Here's to moms - all of us. None of whom are perfect. Here's to our kids who are also perfectly imperfect. We're in this together and so far, so good.

Happy Mother's Day!!

# OUR BETTER ANGELS

THERE'S SO MUCH NOISE right now. It's a constant chatter, buzzing, yelling, throwing insults and memes around as if they could be taken back. Something I learned very early in life is that you can't take certain things back. You can't unsay. Sure apologies are important and sometimes a good argument can even deepen a relationship if both parties can come through the battle having found common ground or built mutual respect. But there has to be a line. There must be a point of basic human decency in which winning is less important than honoring the humanity in the other person.

It would be easy for you to think I was talking about politics in this piece. I'm not. I'm talking about life and the responsibility we have to teach our children that their words have power. Our kids live in a world in which it is very, very easy for them to grow up their entire lives without being held accountable for their speech, how they put their ideas into the world, and how they honor other people's experiences. The internet, social media, etc. make it so that if they don't want to they never have to see the impact of their words. None of us do anymore – BUT – the big difference is that we remember a time when there was accountability and our children do not. This weird new reality is a marker on the timeline of the life of adults who still remember life before Facebook, Instagram, and Snapchat.

I am not a perfect parent by any means. Seriously, not even

close. My kids have way more screen time than I am comfortable with. They talk about things that I don't even understand a little bit. So it's important to you to know that I am not preaching. I struggle with the complex moral and ethical questions of technology and parenting in the strange new reality of the 21st Century as much as anyone.

Making devices the enemy and going off the grid completely isn't realistic – at least not for me. The thing I want to teach my kids most of all is to find the middle way to not live in a world of extremes but the find the path that understands that the confusion, pain, and discomfort in the world is just as important as happiness, meaning, and joy. We don't always get what we want, people don't always see our point of view, and we have to learn to handle disappointment and frustrations without being toxic, vitriolic, jerk faces who stomp and hurl insults when things don't go our way. The internet provides a really interesting – if not exhausting – opportunity to help our kids grapple with the challenges of arguing gracefully, or standing by their beliefs even when others disagree with them – even on the internet (a place where you can ostensibly say whatever you want to whomever you want and have very few repercussions). There can be basic human decency.

I am always reminded of the very insightful quote, of which I do not know the origin "Just because you can do something doesn't mean you should." My job as the mom is to instill the tiny voice in them that is a reminder in those moments that no matter how angry they are, no matter how squarely someone else's words and actions fly in the face of what they know to be correct, real, and of value in this world – there is a right way to say what they want to say. Maybe the right thing means they have to concede in the moment, to agree to disagree, to walk away and live to fight another day with their compassion and decency intact. I am reminded of a very powerful quote originated by Charles Dickens and made famous by Abraham Lincoln "So do the shadows of our own desires stand between us and our better angels, thus their brightness is eclipsed." Winning at all costs is not the answer. The internet challenges that morality in a very deep way. We can look at is as a threat or we can address it as an opportunity. We can remind our children, and ourselves, of our better angels – of the incredible light and beauty and power that exists in every human on this earth even those with whom we fervently disagree. It is possible to fight magnificently and honorably for the things you believe to be right without forgetting the humanity of your enemy. It's hard – a lot harder than yelling insults and attacking people's physical traits, family, or other things that no one has any control over. Let's talk about ideas. Let's disagree. Let's walk away with our heads held high because we didn't allow our better angels to be eclipsed.

In the end, I don't need for my children to believe what I believe or be a mouthpiece for me. What I want is for them to know themselves, to understand their own values in the midst of all of the noise enough to find love and forgiveness in those moments. When you become a parent you have no idea what you are signing up for. It can become so incredibly overwhelming at times that it would almost be easier to take your kids and go live in a hole, but the world needs them to know how to navigate it and we have to find a way to teach them these things that we are only just coming to learn.

# ALL HAIL THE BLUE ONE

I HAVE A HUSBAND AND TWO SONS, therefore I live in a sea of testosterone but my boys are not into sports, instead they love super heroes with an equivalent – if not myopic – level of obsession. My wonderful, loving, supportive, brilliant husband is a comic, excuse me – graphic novel, nerd and this love has rubbed off onto all three kids. Even our daughter would much rather talk about the Marvel universe than the Disney princesses. So instead of fighting against it – I have chosen to embrace this weird little niche and to thank my lucky stars that I am not a football widow. The nerd fest of factoids, upcoming films, new and "exciting" iterations of time honored characters, and retelling of old story lines – though often I'm not sure what the hell they're talking about – have me far more engaged than end zones, fumbles, jump shots and RBI's – wait.. I don't think that's right. Oh well...

The other day I was reading while my boys were watching an episode of *Batman Brave and the Bold*. I usually limit this stuff because while the messages are good they can be a little more violent than I would like. So this was a rare opportunity to engage in this particular show. In the background, I could hear the dialogue and the more I listened the more I was pulled into the show. In this particular episode, Batman and his young sidekick-like fellow super hero Blue Beetle passed through a worm-hole and ended up in another universe with tiny little blob-like beings who found themselves in a certain amount of peril – as is usually the case. Upon seeing the Bat and Beetle the little "blobbies" become very excited and Bat and Beetle automatically assume they must know the Dark Knight on this planet and are happy to have him arrive and save them from their troubles. However, it quickly becomes clear as the creatures gather around Blue Beetle that he is the one they believe is their hero and they chant, "All hail the blue one! All hail the blue one!" Beetle is caught off guard and quickly reminds them that he isn't the hero here – Batman is the hero they've been looking for. Well for all of his Jedi mind-tricking (Yes, I am aware that's from another movie) he can't convince these little guys that he's not their Beetle. Batman, being the good leader that he is stands back and encourages the Beetle to step up, to become the hero that these little alien creatures think he is. I'll let you draw your own conclusions or seek out this episode on Netflix but I think you can figure out what happens in the end.

Of course this got me thinking about heroism in its many forms but mostly in the everydayness of life. When we become parents, we are a little like the Blue Beetle: reticent to make the hard choices, afraid of our certain failure and equally terrified of our power. In this new world we are the ultimate giver of life, care, love, discipline, and dinner – every day forever. The older our kiddos get the more often we are faced with situations in which we have to do "what's in their best interest" even when they are sure we hate them and our only goal in life is to ruin theirs. This morning I found myself walking through the house saying very loudly, "I am sorry to be the mean awful person who makes you wear clothes and eat food!" After the meltdowns and the craziness were done we had a talk in which I said I loved them and it wasn't my job to make everyone happy all the time. It's my job to make sure they know how to do the things they need to do so they can grow up and live in the world. I'm certain that they only heard about half of what I said but when the talk was over I got hugs. We all said, "I love you" without being forced or threatened so I consider that a success. I will build my house with the bricks of tiny wins.

#2 recently did his first play. He gets nervous doing new things. I presented him with the opportunity to try it and gave him a couple of weeks to mull it over. One day he walked into the kitchen and said "I think I want to do that play."

It was a role in a children's choir so he wouldn't have to be alone on stage and that made him feel more comfortable.

"It's going to be a lot of work." I made sure to tell him. "You have to rehearse a lot, sometimes later than your used to being awake, and then you have to get up and go to school the next morning."

"Ok, that's fine," he replied.

"It's a big commitment," I told him, "but it's totally worth it when you see what you've done in the end."

He said he understood and he still wanted to do it. Ok, I thought, here we go.

This is a kid who is super sensitive and easily overwhelmed. He feels the weight of the world in everything he does. I know this kid very well. He is me.

When I was a kid I quit everything. I couldn't handle it. Homework made me meltdown, friends gave me panic attacks, I had stage fright but an overwhelming compulsion to perform. I don't blame anyone for letting me quit - I was exhausting. Yet, I remember all too well the pain and disappointment I would feel after giving up. Because of that experience I have always been very keen to not let my kids quit things because they are scary or overwhelming.

They have certainly walked away from extracurriculars because they lacked interest but for things that are just scary - no way. Getting to the end and facing that fear is the only option. I remember the alternative all too well and it haunted me for far too long.

He started rehearsal and things went incredibly well. He really loved it, was excited to go even in the evening and on weekends.

And then the dancing started.

I had told him it would just be singing because that's what I thought. I was wrong. Don't worry, he didn't let me forget.

After the first choreography rehearsal he was done. He hated it and never wanted to go back. There were only 8 kids in the group and I told him they were counting on him and he had to see it through. I just kept reminding him that I told him it was hard but the pay-off is well worth it.

He begged, cried, yelled, told me I was the meanest person ever, asked me why I hated him and wanted him to be unhappy. He got sick for an entire week of rehearsal and I still wouldn't let him quit. I just kept kissing the top of his head and telling him it would be over soon and he would see. I was more patient as a parent in this process than I have ever been collectively over the course of my entire life. It was really hard.

Then came the day when we got to the first run-through. The kids in #2's group had only been rehearsing the few bits that they were in and had not been around the rest of the cast very much, nor had they seen the entire show. We sat in the back of the theatre on the day of the run through and he and his other young cast mates watched the show. They were mesmerized.

He walked up to me halfway through and said "Now I get it. This is awesome." Of course I cried. He went back to his group with enthusiasm and I breathed a sigh of relief.

Awww, what a nice story. Then we galloped off into the sunset and he made it to Broadway. That did not happen. He still had days when he was tired and gave me a hard time but he made it through to the end. He's not sure he wants to do it again. It really doesn't matter. The super-sensitive, worrier kid showed-up to a thing he had never done before, learned how to do it, sat in his discomfort - had to push through it, then discovered the thing was fun, and he could do it. Wow.

In this experience I just had to be focused on what I knew the outcome would be for him. I had to give him what I wish I had gotten when I was a kid.

Because here's the other thing about that episode of *Batman Brave and the Bold* – the part when Batman stepped aside and LET Blue Beetle find his "hero-ness." That's how it happens in a family – someone let us go into the world either by choice or by necessity, or both, and we had to find it on our own. We have to also let our children find it for themselves – even when they're scared and uncertain – especially then. We have to keep challenging ourselves to find it in new ways and we have to get out of the way of others. That's a huge and powerful gift – letting others find out how strong they are.

Parenting is so much like the Blue Beetle with the blobbies –

we showed up expecting one party and ended up in another one. Only this party asks a lot more of us. I was not Batman – I didn't have the resources at first or the knowledge, the strength or the courage.

So as you go forth into your day try to find opportunities to be someone's Batman and find your inner Blue Beetle.

---

"You've got to jump off cliffs all the time and build your wings on the way down."

**Ray Bradbury**

---

# 10 THINGS THEY DON'T TELL YOU ABOUT BECOMING A PARENT

THEY TELL YOU ABOUT teething, sleep training, milestones, "terrible twos", puberty, and you hear whispers about challenges but there are no specifics! They don't tell you the things you really need to know. Probably because if they did, none of us would be here right now.

10. You'll never be alone again. And quiet will take on a whole new meaning.

9. Bedtime will be the ultimate test of human will, strength and mental acuity. Screw you Mensa and NASA – the smartest people alive are the parents who can get children to go to sleep without yelling, pleading, or complaining – every single night forever...and ever.

8. The passage of time is fluid. Children grow up so incredibly quick – years pass like moments and yet a day alone with a toddler can feel like a thousand years.

7. You will negotiate pants. This is a thing that happens all the time. Not which pants but the wearing of pants, period. We have to wear them everyday and yet I have to remind these people of this far more frequently than I could have ever imagined.

6. You can never imagine the amount of resentment you could have for certain words or questions. Like: "What do you want for dinner?", or "Mommy?"

5. Certain things will come out of your mouth that you can't imagine anyone has ever said before like – "Don't drink from the dog bowl," "don't lick the car," and "don't pee in your sister's suitcase."

4. What is the appropriate protocol when your 9 year old removes his fake mustache at the restaurant table? When my middle son wore a fake mustache to the pizza restaurant last summer, the pizza arrived, and he stuck it to the table. I was in that moment as perplexed as I have ever been regarding what the proper etiquette is for how to handle that situation. Do you know?

3. You will have to tell them *every time* you get into the car to buckle up, the right way! Then you will have to remind them to get out of the car when you've arrived at your destination.

2. You will have moments of pride, moments of bliss, and moments in which you feel pretty good about the how you're doing at this parenting thing. They are only moments. They don't last long then you go back to hoping really hard that however you're screwing them up will wear off in time for them to start changing your diapers.

1. You could never imagine that anything with this level of aggravation, fear, exhaustion, and uncertainty could be so frigging amazing.

# JEFF THE DOG: A SAGA FOR THE AGES

---

"The times when you feel you are most prepared the Universe will throw you a curve ball. Once you've unfurled yourself from the fetal position life goes on – windows or not."

**Erin Mahone**

---

HE WAS BIG AND DARK – handsome and distinguished...a man's dog. We turned the corner in the room at the SPCA, and the moment he saw us he began hopping up and down and talking to us.

"Hello!!!!" his happy face said.

"Here I am. THE ONE you've been waiting for all these years!"

Here he is in the little room at the SPCA.

I told my daughter when she was 3 that we would get a dog – when she was 10. I held firm to that promise over the years. When the promise was made I was certain that we would be done having children by that time, and unlike so many other things I was certain of in my 20's, this was actually true. We were a month away from the little woman's 11th birthday so she was still 10 but time was running out. We piled into the car the day after we had returned from a week at the beach. We were *just going to look at the SPCA* – just see what was out there.

"We are NOT getting a dog today!" I told them all before we went in. Famous last words...

So when we turned that fateful corner and saw that happy boy the children got very excited.

"Can we visit with him?" they asked.

"Please!!??"

Keith and I looked at each other – each of us reticent but also a little smitten.

"Did you see his name?" I asked quietly through my teeth as we conferred.

"Yes" he said "I saw."

"Seems kind of serendipitous – huh?" I said

"It would be pretty funny" he replied.

Why you ask is his name of any significance? Well his name was Jeff – my husband and I each have a brother named Jeff. His older, mine younger but "Jeffs" nonetheless – and we couldn't help but get a little giddy at the silliness of the whole situation. We were being worn down.

We requested a visit with "Jeff – the dog" as we quickly began referring to him. We entered one of those small rooms where your little doggie dreams flash before your eyes. My husband – who was the least ready for the dog – immediately began thinking aloud of the Santa hats Jeff would don and this man's dog sleeping by the fire (on a bear skin rug no doubt, followed by "Tim Taylor" style grunts of manliness). The children were immediately won over. The moment the dog arrived in the room he began licking the children's faces and snuggling up to them. We were pretty psyched to have found this loving guy.

When the adoption counselor came into the room she said a lot of vague things – that looking back were probably warnings but not very effective ones. She said that he was only interested in people – he didn't seem to want to eat or play with toys but he was motivated by interactions with humans. She told us that because he had only been with them a few days it was likely because he was confused about why he was there and feeling afraid.

The thing is when you decide on a rescue animal you have to be prepared for a certain amount of uncertainty because you have no real idea of the animal's experience prior to meeting them. But I was raised on rescues – my mom has been rescuing animals for more than 20 years. We had dogs that ate entire sofas, hid under beds for months at a time, 20 cats with feline leukemia that had been abandoned on the side of the road. We rescued them and they lived in the garage. Our house was a revolving door of animals in need of homes. Some came and went quickly others stayed permanently. I was not some naive first time pet owner who didn't realize how much work an animal is. I was confident that with this rescue training we could handle any eventuality.

The Universe responded to that confidence with hilarious fits of laughter.

Seeing Jeff in action he appeared perfect. He was affectionate and obedient. He loved the children and they loved him. They all looked at me with big begging eyes.

"Can we get him?" they said.

"We weren't going to get a dog today" I replied "We're just looking."

I looked over at my husband who was pretty smitten and we sat there looking at each other trying to be responsible, trying to make the right decision. I was concerned that he was too big – at that moment it was my only concern. We live in a small house that is not really big enough for our family of 5 but he seemed so sweet and it's not easy to find a pet who meshes so well with three lively children. AND his name was Jeff – I mean seriously – JEFF! After all the years of waiting until the right time to get a dog we seemed to have stumbled upon the perfect one for us. So we said yes and we took Jeff home.

He immediately fit in. We made him a spot on the floor and gave him his food and water bowl in the kitchen by the table. He really listened, was house trained, loved the kids, and seemed very mellow – for 18 hours.

We brought Jeff home at 4:30 pm on Sunday. The kids started camp on Monday morning at 9 am and I had to go to work. Now my husband works from home so he would be able to be with Jeff during the transition period but on this Monday morning I had to be at work early. We were just returning from vacation and I had a meeting. So I left and Keith took the kids to camp. He was gone for about an hour. There was a short conversation about not loving the idea of leaving the dog alone as we hadn't gotten a crate yet but Keith would only be gone for a little while and whatever mess Jeff made we would deal with.

At 9:30 am I get a call at my desk from the SPCA. I answered the phone.

"Hi Erin, this is 'Allison' from the SPCA. Do you know where Jeff is?"

"Hi Allison – what do you mean? Jeff is at home."

"No – he isn't. Someone found him wandering down the road. I have the man's name and he says Jeff is fine. Can you go get him?"

"WHAT?! He's been alone for only a few minutes – I don't understand. I don't even know how he could have gotten out. He was in the living room. My husband just ran the kids to camp and to the post office I'm sure he'll be home any minute."

She gave me the man's phone number and I called Keith. "What do you mean he got out?! How did he get out?!" he said when I called.

"I don't have any idea. Can you call the guy and go get the dog?" I replied – both of us near hysterical.

Keith went and got Jeff and called me immediately to report that Jeff was fine and the man who had him was our neighbor down the street. The guy mentioned that Jeff seemed to be bleeding a little bit but he couldn't tell from where. He suggested that we take him to the vet. Keith said he was on his way home and when they got in the house he would call me back.

Crisis averted I thought. Back to work.

No more than five minutes later Keith called back. "You wanna know how Jeff got out of the house?"

From the tone of his voice it didn't sound like I wanted to know but he told me anyway.

"He jumped out of the living room window."

"I'm sorry, what?" I replied

"The window, he jumped out of the living room window. Through two pains of glass. Chewed up the window sill and the front door frame. And there's blood everywhere."

I sat stunned as if I was there but not there – this out-of-body-ness would become my state of being for the next several days.

"You said the neighbor said he was bleeding. Is he bleeding? We need to take him to the vet. Do you see any blood. We don't even have a vet yet. Did you find the blood?" I just rambled everything that I was thinking while my husband searched the dog for blood and no doubt cursed the entire process.

Did I mention this was our second day back from a week at the beach?

"There's a little blood but I'm not sure where it's from. He must have cut himself on the glass from the window."

"Ok, let's just run him over to the vet at the SPCA and maybe they will be willing to look at him – or help us – since we just brought him home. I'll meet you over there." I hung up the phone told my colleagues the quick version of the story and ran out the door. I got to the SPCA and asked for the girl who had worked with us the day before. She was glad we found the dog and sympathetic but they weren't thrilled to help us as this isn't what they do. But before Jeff got there they agreed to look him over. That flew immediately out the door the second Keith arrived at the SPCA with the dog in the back seat of the car. When I ran out and flung open the door it looked like the car in one of those old gangster movies where someone gets shot and bleeds out in the back seat. There was blood everywhere...I ran inside and asked for a towel, ran back out and got the dog from the car walking him in holding the towel under his face. The blood was coming from his face.

All the while he was smiling and happy looking at me as if to say "Hi!! I'm so happy to see you! I really missed you! How has your day been?"

The second we walked into the SPCA clinic they explained they were not equipped to accommodate this situation and sent us to the veterinary hospital a few miles away. So we took the dog and the towel and got back into the car. We ran him into the hospital and they took one look at him and rushed to get him back. We spent the entire rest of the day there. In a state of utter shock, fear for him and deep sadness. I was very, very sad. Just so sad.

While I sat alone at the veterinary hospital all day I just kept saying over and over again to myself, "We waited until we were ready."

WE WAITED NEARLY 8 YEARS!

I mean, shit!

The kids were all old enough to help. They were willing to walk him, feed him, play with him, even pick-up his poop! We had given them trial runs with cousin dogs and their grandmother's dogs. We had a yard and a quiet cul-de-sac. I cried a lot that day.

When he finally came out all stitched up – 14 stitches in his right cheek – we went home. Thank goodness for generous parents who offered to help with the massive vet bill! I dropped him with the family and immediately ran to buy a crate. I got the biggest one and went home. We put it together and he immediately – as if this was what had been missing – hopped inside and fell asleep. Our first 24 hours with Jeff the dog had come to an end. It seemed as if we were going to be ok.

The kids were terrified and saddened by this turn of events. Our daughter was so upset she couldn't look at him without crying. The other two gently petted and hugged him. They all wanted to understand why he had done this. We tried to explain that sometimes dogs, and people, don't get what they need from the people who are supposed to take care of them and when that happens it can make them act out in scary or dangerous ways.

We went to bed that night exhausted but hopeful that though our beginnings with Jeff the dog were rocky we would be able to find our footing and go forward on the road to pet ownership with all the bad behind us. I was raised by a mom who rescued animals. I had spent my youth and young adulthood dealing with dogs and cats that had many different emotional challenges – a lot like the people in our family. They found their home with us. Maybe we understood them. I felt like they got what they needed from my mom who just loved them all to pieces. I was sure that I was prepared for a life as a rescue parent.

The next day Jeff lay around and seemed to be getting used to us. He was very nervous and would whine when we left the room even just to go to the bathroom. The kids were very anxious around him but they really loved him and wanted to help him to feel comfortable. We were feeling more hopeful – cautiously optimistic. We reinforced the crate with zipties and Jeff seemed really comfortable in it. I had slept on the sofa since the accident in order to help him get comfortable with his new home, his crate and the many staples in his face complete with a cone of shame.

On Wednesday morning I left for work and took the kids to camp. My husband put Jeff inside his new crate and left for less than an hour to run some errands. Then I got the call...again.

"Hello" I said.

"He did it again." It was my husband on the other end of the phone this time.

"What do you mean? I left him in the crate. I tied the thing together!"

"He broke out of it and he jumped through the other window." My husband informed me.

"What?!?! How?!?!" I screamed.

"I don't know. I don't have any idea. The crate is completely bent up. I don't know how he did it," he replied.

"We can't do this. We have to take him back, Erin. We aren't prepared to care for this dog. He needs another dog. He can't be left alone ever – not even for us to sleep or go to the bathroom. It's not fair to him or us."

He said it and I knew he was right but I just started to cry. I felt like a failure. It was awful. I worried about what to tell the children and what this would mean for future dog ownership. I went into a friends' office at work and told him what was happening and about my concerns regarding what to tell the kids.

"Harry and the Hendersons" he said confidently as if I was supposed to know what that meant. Obviously, I remembered the movie from my childhood but, though Jeff the dog was unstable, he wasn't big foot.

"Huh?" I asked.

"Harry wanted to be with the Hendersons and the Hendersons wanted Harry but it couldn't work. He was too big and unpredictable and they weren't equipped to meet his needs. The best thing they could do for Harry and their family was to let him go. It was awful and hard but in the end it was the only choice they had."

"Woah. That was the best thing anyone could have said to me right now. Thanks man" I responded to his perfect insight. It made me feel better. Not completely better, but better. Someone else could make it work. I still think that. I just wish I was the person who could have made it work, but I'm not. We have three kids and full time jobs. I thought I was ready – we were ready. I was wrong. What a way to learn that lesson. I still feel a little like a failure, like I let that poor guy down. That probably won't ever go away.

Almost a year to the day passed but the opportunity arose once again to grow our family with a dog. This time a friend of mine's neighbor had puppies and she was trying to help find homes for them. There were two left, a boy and a girl.

When we went to visit the kids sat in the driveway. The little boy puppy barked and yapped at us the entire time but wouldn't come near. The little girl calmly walked over to #2 and curled up in his lap. We took her home with us that day. She was a sandy, scraggly, 8 pound little mutt that wouldn't get much bigger, and puked in the car on the way home. It couldn't get much worse than Jeff but I was hoping she wouldn't prove me wrong. It took almost the entire day to agree on a name but when I (*note: *my husband insists it was him*) said "What about Kismet?" everyone said "That's it!" even though they had no idea what the word meant. Kismet means fate, destiny. She was certainly meant for us.

I was taught growing up that a pet is a member of the family. The responsibility to care for them is as big as it is for any human

– maybe even more. I never thought I would have to return a dog. This process was beyond anything I could have imagined. I wasn't sure we would ever be ready to be pet parents again. This was just one of a thousand times during the course of life as mom, wife, person on the planet when I have expected one thing only to be faced with something entirely different. We tried, as we always do, to make the right decision. Some decisions are easier than others. When you're a grown-up you have to make the hard choices even when you don't want to.

Even though Jeff the mostly free dog from the SPCA cost us over $3000 and long lasting emotional scars in the 55 hours he was a part of our family I am still glad we decided to bring him home with us. I could have done without all the blood and the staples in his face but in the end we all learned some pretty valuable lessons about ourselves and our family. Sometimes things aren't right even when we really want for them to be. Jeff the dog will always be listed among our family pets. He made a lasting impression and we only wanted the best for him.

# PURSUIT OF SANITY

# I STARTED ON A TUESDAY

---

*"The first time I see a jogger smiling, I'll consider it."*

**Joan Rivers**

---

MY HUSBAND AND I have a running joke about starting new things that goes a little like this:

ME: Honey, let's train to climb Mt. Everest.

HIM: Ok, sure! That sounds great. We'll start on Monday.

OR

ME: Honey, let's take a class on Indigenous Cultures!

HIM: Absolutely! When I get skinny, we can totally do that.

At which point, I know whatever it is that I've proposed will never happen. As we enter into the 16th year of our relationship, I realize there are many different elements at work in these interactions.

1. I am a little nuts.

2. He loves me in spite of the looniness.

3. He doesn't like change.

4. I like it too much.

5. He is very good at avoiding an argument by using humor.

6. I am a little nuts.

7. I have an enormous amount of enthusiasm – for everything.

8. He loves me anyway.

9. He is very unhealthy, stubborn and unmotivated.

10. I love him anyway.


So in our commitment to our relationship, and, our family, and our respect for one another, we have made the unspoken agreement to engage in this interaction – forever. Lately though, I've been thinking a lot about our physical and emotional health, that of our children, and how to manage the immensely difficult task of being in 43 places at once. With mental illness and disease running rampant through our families I would like to live healthier because there is much to be done and it's easier to get it all done when I'm not sick, and exhausted all the time.

You see, I am super excited to be alive on this planet and there are many things that I have done and thousands more things I have yet to do. I want to do them all. The problem is that I have the passion of 10,000 Italian men and the attention span of a squirrel. So we continue to engage in this way; I make a grandiose suggestion and he knows that the desire to do this thing will likely pass within the hour so he agrees – sort of.

I have always felt as if I am in a race against time to get everything done. The problem is when I think about all of the things that I want to do in life, I get so overwhelmed by the magnitude and so disheartened by the time that I have wasted that I end up doing nothing. For instance, if I want to watch a movie I look at the list of movies. That starts me thinking about all the movies in the world. Then I get so upset about the fact that I have not seen them all that I cannot choose just one – so I just turn on HGTV or listen to NPR. The same goes for books, music, musicals, artists, philosophy and religion. I want to learn everything but because I don't already know it all I get angry with myself and then I just put it off until – Monday. Or when I get skinny.

But one morning in the shower I decided that there is no time like the present. I am not skinny and today is Tuesday. So what - here I go! I'm breaking the mold. I'm stepping out. Today is the day. I have struggled with anxiety and depression my entire life. I have watched mental health challenges destroy many people around me and I have watched fear destroy even more. I have seen so many people, including myself wait to start their lives until something else happens or for the perfect beginning. It never comes. Conversely, I have also seen others whom I admire greatly push through their fear, self-doubt, and depression to achieve great success. So I ask why the hell can't I do that for myself? Tuesday is the day - and Wednesday, Thursday, Friday, and so on. It's time to recognize that life is short, being happy is work, and it's a choice. Not just today, but everyday. I can do whatever I want so now it's time to figure out what that is and go for it.

Life is filled with uncertainty. The only thing we control is our reaction, our commitments, and our choices. I want to be healthy, feel better, and get in touch with the part of me that has gotten lost somewhere along the way. The me that once did crafts just because, listened to music, sang in the car, took walks, and drank coffee outside every morning. I want to rid myself of the pit of fear that has been lodged in my gut for years. I want to take control, and really start enjoying my life. I want to write, perform, and help others. I want to be a great mom and an awesome wife. I want to be the best me possible. I want to make conscious choices. I want to really live. Today is the first step on that journey. I am starting where I am to get where I want to go.

## First Yoga in years....

Walked into class to find the Rabbi's wife, a co-worker, and then the Rabbi, who came in and sat right in front of me. The thoughts of this being a relaxing endeavor were replaced with thoughts of "do my feet smell?", "are they too close to his head?", "do I look like a total moron?", "is she better at this than me?", "please don't fart. please don't fart..." but somehow I managed to keep going. Now I feel like a bowl of jell-o, but I think I'll go back tomorrow.

## Day 2

Ok, so I've been faithfully devoted to a cleaner, healthier lifestyle now for over 36 hours...why is there still cellulite on my upper arms and thighs?! Why do I not have a beautiful mind?!

I worked out again today. It was just 35 minutes on the elliptical, 2.5 miles and 215 calories burned. That's ok. But I am in so much pain. Not to mention not getting enough sleep last night because we had to stay up until 1 am discussing the ins and outs of TV superheroes and their appropriateness for the children... and other exciting topics of interest...such as: Why you're wrong and I'm not!; What does that mean?; Don't be so emotional!; But What you Really Meant Was, also known as That's Not What I Said, and so many more. Marriage is fun.

I peed a lot today. Probably from all the water and smoothies I've been drinking. Every time I have to stop what I'm doing and run to the bathroom, I try to think about all the fat, toxins, and evil demons I'm releasing from my body. It helps to keep me drinking – which is a challenging task. Some days, I come home from working 8 – 10 hours or more and I realize that I didn't drink anything all day except coffee!

## Day 3

The third day is always the worst. I hurt. Everywhere. I'm still feeling impatient because the total body/mind transformation is not complete but I'm definitely feeling better...even with the pain. I finally found my scale this morning – yes, I lost - or perhaps temporarily misplaced - my scale but I found it under my bed. Whatever, shut up!

It read 6 lbs. more than I expected so I guess this whole endeavor was appropriately timed if not planned. Surprisingly, this morning I woke up after a 13 hour day yesterday and facing another 12+ hour day today and I don't feel as if I'm going to die. Generally, I wake up following one of those long days with an excruciating headache that gets worse throughout the day. Today I feel tired and sore but it's manageable and I feel pretty good.

But here's the biggest thing – and I'm never sure what is related to what but mentally I'm sharper, and emotionally I'm more balanced. Last night, I got upset about something that my husband did. I was frustrated and I withdrew until this morning. But when he finally asked me about it, I was able to say, "That situation upset me but I honestly don't know who was in the right. I am feeling that we aren't communicating very well lately and I would like us to make more of an effort to be kinder to one another." He agreed and there was no argument. If that was caused by this new conscious approach I am happy to report it. If it is totally unrelated then it's still worth noting. I feel better. That's good.

### Day 4 with several days off the wagon...

I fell miserably off the wagon. It's true. I worked two 12+ hour days last week and I couldn't muster the energy to continue on the right track. I have been eating at night, not working out, and basically not doing anything but working and mothering. Instead of losing 20 lbs., I've gained 5 and I am completely burned out. I began this little endeavor weighing 6 lbs. more than I thought I did and so essentially, I've gained 11 lbs. over the last 9 days. That's what I call success!

And here is where the reality lies: Life is hard and I am not perfect. I am good, sometimes I am great, but most of the time I'm just doing the best I can in the moment. I'm almost always a nice person and treat people with respect. I am generous with my love and my time – most days. I am not always good at saying no, being good to myself, or avoiding cookies at 10 pm. I am not patient – with anyone – including my kids and my husband. This is the thing I need to work on most – and the not eating cookies at 10 pm thing...and about a thousand other things but these are bugging me most today. Being a grown-up is a lot harder than I thought it would be.

# FAILING AT NIRVANA

---

"I equate ego with trying to figure everything out
instead of going with the flow. That closes your heart
and your mind to the person or situation that's right in
front of you, and you miss so much."

**Pema Chodron**

---

D ID YOU KNOW that it's hard looking stupid? Well there you go. If you didn't know I have now informed you as such. Looking dumb sucks! I try to avoid it at all costs. One morning when I walked into a Yoga/Pilates fusion class carrying the confidence that I generally walk into my regular yoga class with I was completely unprepared. The Pilates part used muscles that I put to sleep long ago. Yes, they likely needed to awaken but I forgot they were sleeping and they weren't ok with me waking them up. It hurt. I have no core strength and at one point the instructor had to stand next to me and hold me up so I didn't face plant. She kept smiling, laughing, making jokes and talking to people during the class. This made me very angry. Everyone was having fun.

I was looking for a meditative experience, peaceful and quiet, with breathing and slow movement. I began the day with an expectation that – "This will take me to the next level of experience and I will become enlightened. I will then leave this space and enter into my work day with focus, clarity, and a glow that says - I am adulting effectively! I am two yoga sessions and a meditation away from frigging nirvana."

You see, I have been on a bit of a journey of late. I am feeling spiritually deprived. Last week, while I was on vacation, I began to fill this void with meditation apps and podcasts, listening to interviews with Rabbis, Mystics, Gurus, Yogis, Maharajis. I was reading about Kabbalah, Ayurveda, Jewish Renewal, Buddhism, etc. I decided that it is time to deepen my meditation practice, go back to yoga on a regular basis, become more mindful. I'm working very seriously on this. It's very serious. It's time to get peaceful. Damn it!

As I sat twisted like a pretzel and fearing for my physical safety, the reality of my epic nirvana failure fully sunk in. I couldn't help screaming inwardly, "Why the f@*k is she so damn loud!" I was uncomfortable, my muscles were shaking, I kept falling down, and I wanted my moment of Zen. People were sitting on their elbows for God sake! She periodically commented on the sourpusses in the room. I knew she was talking about me and it made my puss even sourer. That sounded dirty but I'm leaving it in because I am a grown-up and I can do what I want.

I chose this class because it's the only one I could fit into my work day without taking away time with my family. I wanted my regular yoga class – which is quiet and peaceful and challenging without making me afraid of facial lacerations and a possible concussion. I had to get it done and check this whole enlightenment thing off my list so I can get on with the business of living. I have other shit to do. But the regular classes were just too late in the day so I figured, "How different could it be? Yoga is yoga, right?"

Ha.

I began to reflect on all the listening that I did last week. Those long, quiet walks in the park reflecting on where I am and where I want to be. The interviews I listened to with great spiritual leaders who all said the same thing – love is the only thing. Find a way to not be reactionary, but to be present, to experience whatever I'm feeling, acknowledge it, and figure out what it's trying to tell me about myself in this moment.

In that moment, I felt silly, not at all relaxed, and very weak. I was reminded that a broken pelvis and 3 pregnancies had made my body a mess and I can't ignore it anymore. It's not what I went there to learn about myself today. There was a plan. Yoga/Pilates was not sticking to my plan. Stomps, crosses arms, and pouts.

But in the face of the discomfort and disappointment I did something I've never done before. I started listening – remembering all that stuff I had been taking in over the last week – and it occurred to me that the joy this woman was sharing with this class was exactly the right thing. Her playful energy, though irritating to me in the moment, was the lesson I needed to learn. Finding joy in the moment was the point. Deciding that I was going to enjoy myself no matter how different the outcome was from my expectations. That's the real journey, right? I wasn't there to do something so that I could check off a box. I was there to be challenged because putting myself in those uncomfortable situations is where the growth happens. When I can react positively to unexpected struggle, then I have learned the lesson.

Well, I'm not there yet, so I guess I'll have to go back again on Wednesday.

---

"Everybody is a genius. But if you judge a fish by its
ability to climb a tree, it will live its whole life believing
that it is stupid."

**Albert Einstein**

---

# BEING A GROWN-UP IS HARDER THAN I THOUGHT IT WOULD BE

"As a child I assumed that when I reached adulthood, I would have grown-up thoughts."

**David Sedaris**

I FIND THAT AT TIMES I am my own worst enemy, I suppose that is true of many people but this is especially true in circumstances when I know the most positive outcome will arise from taking a certain action or refraining from others. After the birth of my third child, and before the insanity of having three children fully set-in, I wrote the following, I call it my "Mommy Mantra":

*Today is my day. I will shower, eat well, and do some form of exercise, however little. I will kiss my husband. I will play with my children. I will make time for kindness and generosity. Not out of pride or fear but because of a genuine desire to serve and make the world a better place. I will not forget my friends, or the things I love that make me who I am. I will be all of myself a little at a time. I will give love and accept love. Most of all, I will be grateful for the abundance in my life and do my best to earn it each and every day. I will breathe deeply and exhale.*

How poetic, how idealistic, how filled with love, hope, and garbage... The fact of the matter is that sometimes we just want to eat cookies and play Candy Crush – for like a month.

Yet, the little voice in the back of our heads – call it what you will, conscience, inner voice, the great green guilt monster – reminds us to stop eating those cookies and get to the business of living. We know what to do to ensure the very best outcome – and occasionally eating cookies and playing Candy Crush is exactly what we need at that moment – but deep down we know when enough is enough – we hear that voice and we have a choice to make.

I know for myself that when I am getting ready to go on stage, the best thing I can do for my performance is to warm-up completely, take time to breathe and focus, think about all the things I have to do, and get my anxiety in check. Still, there are times when I am driving to a gig listening to a really cool podcast rather than warming up, or instead of getting centered, I am socializing before the show – hanging out, and not doing what would inevitably make the performance, and ultimately my experience, the best it can possibly be. Sometimes I'm just tired. Well, to be honest I'm always tired, sometimes I'm just better at sucking it up and getting out of my own way.

This happens for me, and I imagine a few of you, in virtually every area of my life at some point, fitness, food, work, family – procrastination is the word I think. Waiting. For what? I dunno. Look I never said I was perfect.

I digress, the reality is that we all do this to some degree – some of us more than others – we lament on there not being enough time, energy, or resources. I have a friend who is a recovering heroin addict. He has a really interesting perspective on the concept of not having enough time to do the things they want to do, like writing in particular. He explains that he has little sympathy for that argument. If being a junkie taught him anything, it was time management and focusing on a goal. He had to make $250 per day to support his habit. If he could be a junkie and still figure out how to do that then we can find time to write for 30 minutes, or exercise, practice piano, read a book – whatever the goal."

We think about what isn't happening and yet we also try to cram way more into a day, week, month, year, than is reasonable or sane. There are days when I am very good at acting in my own best interest. There are days – few and far between – when I in fact do all of the things in that Mommy Mantra, even showering, but I can promise you that is not the case most of the time. I won't give up though.

There is a lot of advice in the world these days – a lot of blogs, books, and TV shows telling us that our lives would be better if we all just made that individual's prescribed choices. I'm not telling anyone how to do life because I don't have a clue. All I'm saying is give yourself a break, listen to the inner voice, try not to let it turn into a great green guilt monster, and if you have a bad day – don't worry because tomorrow is another chance.

# GROWING UP IN A MODERN FAMILY: MY EXODUS INTO TRADITIONAL TERRITORY

---

"I have woven a parachute out of everything broken. "

**William Stafford**

---

UNTIL WE WERE TEENAGERS, my brother and I were shuffled back and forth among parents and grandparents while the wide world of options were entertained by our parents. And now I have a couple of former step-parents and step-siblings that I'm friends with on Facebook; yet another generational phenomenon that my children are cataloging for the future when they will write books about how my life choices scarred them in various ways. I realize it all moves full circle and for this little book I will be rewarded handsomely with "payback". And you know what they say about payback...

My parents were also one of the first generations to begin marrying en masse between religions. I have the distinct honor of being a southern Baptist Jew. The two cancel each other out so until I was a mother and made a choice for myself I was – in fact – nothing.

My brother and I began our lives as part of a fairly mundane sociological experiment. An experiment, in our case, that went moderately awry. I am merely a statistic (or casualty) of the late 70's early 80's modern approach to raising a family. And the answer to the hypothesis, or the beginning of a tired joke, is that when an 18 year old Jew, and a 20 year old southern Baptist - with only their shared experience of family mental illness in common - they don't have the skills necessary to cope with marriage and its challenges. Who knew?

When it was time for me to put my life into action, it seemed that the only direction in which I could go was toward creating a family that made sense, and that worked. But what the hell did that look like? Until I was 25 years old I had an irrational fear of grocery stores and I ran out of gas in bad neighborhoods at least twice a year! How could I become someone who folded fitted sheets? I am ashamed to admit that I once told someone that when I ran out of clean underwear, I just threw them all away and bought new ones. How could that person learn how to keep small humans alive? Yet, that's all I ever really wanted – to create the family that I had always longed for.

# REMEMBERING WHAT'S REALLY IMPORTANT

---

"Write it on your heart that every day is the best day in the year."

**Ralph Waldo Emerson**

---

A FEW NEW YEAR'S RESOLUTIONS:

1. Lose 20 pounds.

2. Be more present.

3. Be more patient with my kids.

4. Leave fewer coffee cups in my car.

5. Get more sleep.

6. Eat healthier.

7. Exercise to improve thyroid function.

8. Clean every inch of my house from top to bottom, paint all the rooms and organize my closets.

9. Create a better filing system at work.

10. Increase attendance at all of my work events.

11. Be a more consistent parent.

12. Have more energy.

13. Make more time for friends.

14. Date my husband.

15. Have more sex. (Per that article "You Should Be Having Sex 37 times per Day" or maybe it just says every day – either way.)

16. Read more.

17. Don't fall asleep while reading.

18. Try to remember things I've just read.

19. Be a better person.

20. Solve all the world's problems.

21. Wear lipstick.

22. Do more Pinterest parenting: e.g. Anthropomorphize my children's food more frequently.

23. Have more play dates for my kids.

24. Help more.

25. Learn more.

26. Do my one-woman show.

26. Watch all the movies, listen to all the music and know everything all the time. I am convinced this is completely possible with proper planning and discipline.

27. Set attainable goals.


I'm certain there are more. So. Many. More. Things I want to accomplish-to do better. I probably won't do many of these things. Maybe I'll do them for a day, a week, an hour, or I'll think about doing them a lot while doing other things like: eating, sleeping, working, and trying to keep 3 little people alive.

But here's what I AM doing: honoring Holocaust survivors: Connecting great artists with awesome projects; honoring my heritage through the artists telling our stories. I'm telling those stories myself. I'm in a play, my first musical in years in fact, about a little-known story of intolerance and violence that really happened – like so many stories from 100 years ago and 50 years ago and yesterday and hopefully not too many more tomorrows. I'm writing a blog and a book – though not as often as I would like – but the support and the responses I get are what keep me inspired to continue proudly oversharing.

Our kids love going to school. They love to learn and they are independent. They have good friends and interests in things that excite them. They're funny and they're sweet and they're compassionate. When they aren't screaming at each other, watching too much TV and making huge messes that they don't clean up – didn't want you to get the wrong idea – there is no perfection here.

I just celebrated my 14th wedding anniversary with someone whom I really like and who, most days, really likes me back. We have overcome great obstacles together. We provide a safe home for our children. We have established our own family traditions. We document their lives. We all love each other. We support each other's weaknesses and strengths. We go new places and share new experiences. We teach our kids to value education. We have fun. We teach them gently about the injustices of the world in an attempt to make them aware of the power they possess to make the world good, to understand that everybody does not have the same kind of life that they do, to help and to be grateful. All in between the yelling, exhaustion, and messes.

One of my new favorite poems is by Mary Oliver. It's short but it says so much for me right now.

**Instructions for living a life:**

1. Pay attention

2. Be astonished

3. Write about it.

The only thing I would add to that list is – don't be afraid to be fully in the world. Make choices, get involved, speak your mind, do the things you've wanted to do but have made you afraid. I'm always most fulfilled when I have done this.

I guess I really just have one New Year's resolution this year and that is to spend more time focusing on the good that I'm already doing, the abundance with which I have been blessed, and for which I have worked hard. I just did it.

# LIVING LIFE IN ALL CAPS

---

"A lot of people are living with mental illness around them. Either you love one, or you are one."

**Mark Ruffalo**

---

*Anxiety:*

*anx·i·e·ty*

*noun*

*a feeling of worry, nervousness, or unease, typically about an imminent event or something with an uncertain outcome.*

How does this translate to life with anxiety?

An imminent event being the next breath, phone call or face-to-face interaction.

An outcome being everything.

The best way I have come to describe my anxiety is that it's kind of like everything is in all CAPS – ALL THE TIME. I talk in all caps and people ask me why I'm yelling at them. I walk in all caps and people ask me where I'm going in such a hurry. I breathe in all caps and it sounds like I'm in labor.

I've tried my whole life not to let my "crazy" leak out onto others. That usually means keeping everyone at arm's length knowing with certainty no one would actually want to be in my presence if they saw me in all caps too many times. It's exhausting when life is screaming at you all the time. Believe me.

I've finally reached a place, whether through the process of aging, being surrounded by the right people or divine intervention, where I feel less concerned about getting my anxiety on people. It's part of me. A big, big part.

I try to be cool. I'm desperately not cool. I try to be calm. It doesn't work. I try to be everything to everyone, including myself. It never turns out well.

Here are some positive things about anxiety: I care a lot about everything. I will work really hard to make things the way I envision them. I am vulnerable. That's terrifying but somehow it works, as long, as it doesn't come out at the wrong time.

Lastly — I'm strong. It may not always appear that way, but I promise you when every second is as challenging as it is when you live with anxiety, you have to be tough to hold it all together.

What does a person with anxiety need? The same thing as everyone else only sometimes a little more.

It's hard for me to ask for help of any kind. I worry it will be perceived as incompetence, weakness or laziness. It is in those moments of need when I feel the insecurity and inadequacy that comes with anxiety. That little mean voice pops up inside my head — you know it, everyone has it — whispers, "*Someone better than you could do this all by themselves. If you were really all you're cracked up to be you could make this work. You should be able to do this all by yourself.*"

In reaction to that mean little voice I know is full of sh%t, I still dig in. I become resolute to do everything, all by myself. That makes me really tired. It's not a good plan if your goal is longevity, so I'm working on it.

Here's the other thing about that though: Growing up as a kid struggling with anxiety and depression, I failed a lot. I never felt successful. Even when I did good things, I never felt like it was enough to make up for all the places where I had fallen short. So now, even now, every opportunity to feel successful is one I relish and I cherish. It feels good to accomplish something, no matter how small. The success monster has a voracious appetite. He is never sated. I have traded one extreme for another. I make people tired. I've been told that before, "Erin, you make me tired." I think it was meant as a compliment. I tried to take it that way.

It's hard to find people who accept and respect you even in the face of a life in all caps. I don't expect a lot from most people. I'm sensitive and it's hard to let people in when you walk around with no skin. When I do find a person or people who understand, who get me, who don't mind all of the nuttiness — I make sure to keep them in my life.

The older I get, surprisingly, the easier it is for me to let people in. Only a little easier, I still don't invite people into a messy house which is why I rarely have people over... it's always a messy house. I'll happily meet for dinner, drinks, coffee or whatever. I have good friends, way more than I thought I'd ever have, and I love them. I'm learning to let them love me back. It's really hard.

The movement of speaking out about mental health issues is growing. We are teaching the world it's just fine to be sensitive, anxious and "weird." Our diagnoses, no matter how severe, do not define or limit our capacity for greatness, achievement or love.

# LIFE IN PENCIL

---

"Nothing is softer or more flexible than water, yet
nothing can resist it."

**Lao Tzu**

---

A FEW WEEKS AGO while scanning Facebook, I saw a meme
posted by a friend who's an actor. It was something silly
about starting a new play and always being the person in the
cast who forgets to bring a sharpened pencil. You see, the rule
for theatre is you always bring a pencil to rehearsal so you can
change things along the way. The director comes in with an
understanding of the piece, the cast, the stage, but throughout
the process new ideas, opportunities, and challenges are revealed
making it necessary for the actors to take notes in pencil. The
meme was silly and resonated with me because I always feel like
the guy who showed up on the first day filled with enthusiasm
and lacking a pencil.

However, it got me thinking about how fortunate I am to
have been involved with theatre since I was a kid. It was one of
those light bulb moments when I suddenly thought to myself,
"Wow – that whole pencil thing is a pretty incredible mantra for

living a life!" At which point, I heard in my head the voices of my children laughing at me, rolling their eyes and saying, "Mommy, you can make anything into a learning opportunity." They don't mean this in a nice way. Or my husband saying I'm the most analytical person he's ever met and sometimes the walls are red because they're just red – not everything needs to have a deeper meaning. I totally agree that not everything should be broken down into the wisdom nugget of the day...except when it should. So, I pushed aside the contradictory voices in my head and chose instead to listen to the voices saying the deep and meaningful things that I wanted to listen to.

I digress.

I promise not to go too far down the rabbit hole of the theatre metaphor – but trust me all of the really important lessons of life can be learned in the process of putting on a play. Just as a director and cast come to a play with a script in hand and, hopefully, a general idea of their roles based on the words on the page and their own preparation – people come to life, with a framework and a general idea based on their experiences and interactions. There are some things that, no matter what, cannot be changed. The source material is what it is. You may tweak a word here or a stage direction there but ultimately what is on the page has been predetermined and the participants in the production must do their best to work with what is in front of them. You can only do as my mother always says and, "make do with whatcha got!" So as a result you have to be open to using your pencil, adjusting as you go.

Being alive on the planet is hardly a clear cut, easy pursuit. There are certainly those folks who seem to know how to do life particularly well and might be able to go through their entire lives in pen and be just hunky dory. If you are one of those people, then maybe you should be writing this instead of me. I, however, have never encountered a single, solitary human who didn't need, or want, a do-over at least once in their lives. If you bring a pencil and you're ok using it then you have the power to take risks. You have the power to open your mind to all of the possibilities. You don't get tied to "the way it's always been done" because you've got a pencil. With that comes the gift of getting to say "yes." There's so much freedom in that.

Sure, there will be times when you'll commit to a choice and it won't turn out the way you'd expected but in most cases everyone is still alive and you can try again tomorrow. When I had my first child, a little perfect baby girl who immediately slept through the night, loved everyone and was basically born into adulthood, I was stoked to have another baby as soon as possible. I felt certain that I was gifted in the ways of mothering and would no doubt continue producing equally magnificent and easy going off-spring. Well, as you can only imagine, that was a hilarious and incorrect assessment. It took me over a year, after the birth of my second child, to remember all of my limbs and clothing before leaving the house. Shortly into life as a mother of two I had erased everything of which I had been so certain just months before. Then I had a third child and threw out the script entirely. Now I rewrite it daily, in pencil from the start...on paper made of Xanax and held together with my own tears.

When I was very young, I just knew that one day I would be on Broadway. I moved to New York City to live the dream of life as a bartender, who occasionally worked as an actress and singer (badump bump). For the couple of years leading up to that move, as I worked and trained there had been this nagging thought in the back of my mind; that even though I had spent my entire young life preparing for this, and I was born with the ability to sing and do characters, and the people in my life had always told me that's what I would do, should do, was meant to do that I didn't really want to be on Broadway. That's not to say I would have ended up on Broadway, even if I had wanted it more than anyone. It was the realization, after all those years, that I didn't want it was the hardest to accept. This was the make-up of my entire identity. There was nothing else. How could I start over being a person if this wasn't my goal? Fortunately, I had my pencil and started from page one.

Believe me, there were missteps along the way – I spent two years as a terrible real estate agent, not that there's anything wrong with that profession except that I shouldn't be doing it. But I figured some things out. I got married, had my first child and realized that I couldn't be the mother I wanted her to have without finishing my education. I had always wanted to help people and make a difference in the world. So I went back to school and got degrees in social and behavioral sciences and started down a very long path which has led me here. I have lived my life in fits and starts, usually following my instincts rather than a plan. In some areas this has been disastrous, but most of the time it has led to the most beautiful realizations. I know not everyone is as comfortable with the unknown as I tend to be but having a pencil at the ready means that when you are met with disappointment – which is inevitable - instead of a dead end, it's just an opportunity to try another approach.

All we can do is try things. Of course, have a plan, have a belief system, have goals, and be committed to them - that's important and honorable. But my goodness, if in the play that is your life, you keep tripping over a piece of the set, you never have enough time to get from one spot to another, or you're so caught up in the tripping, bumping and rushing that you can't give your emotional all to the role - then talk to the director, take out your pencil and find another way. The thing I've realized is that using the pencil doesn't mean I've failed. It means I've taken a chance, discovered a new truth for myself, and most importantly acknowledged that something isn't working, and I've asked for support in addressing it. The difference between life and a play is obvious – in life, every day is a performance with little to no time for rehearsal. We can never expect more from ourselves, or the people around us than a willingness to learn from our mistakes and to keep trying until we get it right.

# MAKE YOU FEEL MY LOVE

---

"In some families, 'please' is described as the magic word. In our house, however, it was 'sorry'."

**Margaret Laurence**

---

ONE OF MY VERY FAVORITE SONGS both to sing and listen to is "Make You Feel My Love" by Bob Dylan, covered by artists from nearly every genre. It is a timeless love song with remarkable lyrics and a beautiful, simple melody. I've never met someone who didn't like this song. It speaks universally of the depth of one person's love for another – it says what love is:

"When the rain is blowing in your face and the whole world is on your case, I can offer you a warm embrace to make you feel my love...I know you haven't made your mind up yet, but I would never do you wrong I knew right from the moment that we met – no doubt in my mind where you belong...storms are raging on the rolling sea and on the highway of regret the winds of change are blowin' wild and free – but you ain't seen nothin' like me yet...I can make you happy make your dreams come true – no there's nothing that I wouldn't do – go to the ends of the earth for you to make you feel my love."

That's not the whole thing, but you get the gist. It's a lovely song about love. Cut to real life...the place where we actually have to fit our raw emotions – our visions of what would be – into the blender of daily life and sometimes what comes out is not the sweet and genuine statement of "here's what I will do to make you feel how much I love you every day." Instead, we find ourselves forcing our loved ones to chug the "I will make you feel my love if it kills us all!" smoothie of the day. It can be difficult to give our significant others – and often our children even more – the love they need and are most able to accept in a way that is meaningful. Rather, we shove our ideas of what things are "supposed" to feel like, look like, and inevitably what our giving of affection is going to mean to them and about us – down their throats – whether they like it or not! "I will MAKE you FEEL MY love" – and it becomes all about us and ultimately not about love.

At work and in our lives outside these most intimate relationships – for the most part – people have to accept what we have to give. They can make suggestions or demand certain adjustments but overall at the end of the day we all go back to our own corners and while friendships and work interactions are important we have a certain amount of control over how much we are giving to others and they have to take it or leave it.

I entered my adult life with very concrete goals in place about marriage and family – basically that I would conquer them! My point of view came from the way I grew up – a child of multiple divorces, lots of moving, lots of changing schools, and interchangeable step-families, at times not knowing where I was going to live – and often not feeling safe. I knew I could do it better and my husband and children would see how hard I was trying and how much I loved them and they would hoist me on their shoulders and crown me "Queen Mommy and Wife of the Universe." The thing I struggled to realize, that now seems so obvious, is that my husband and children do not share my past. Their framework for life is not built of MY experiences but MY experiences can positively or negatively impact how their framework is built.

Instead of thinking about my needs, goals, expectations, past experiences, wanting to be a better parent and wanting to conquer marriage, what if I just looked at the people around me and completely removed myself from the equation? Is that possible? I would venture to guess that – at least in my life – I would have a lot more patience with everyone in my home if I removed my "stuff" from *their* lives. Who am I to say anymore than that - beyond the expectation that they are kind, healthy, and purposeful?

In the end, making our love for others felt has so much more to do with them than it has to do with us. Love is messy and imperfect just like people. What if we stop trying to fit it in a box, wrap it, label it, and post it on Facebook – and instead we start listening and taking advantage of the little moments to quietly share our love instead of trying "make" others feel it all the time – who knows what could happen?

# THOSE MOMENTS

---

"The butterfly counts not months but moments, and has time enough."

**Rabindranath Tagore**

---

THERE ARE THOSE MOMENTS when I feel in complete relationship with God. I've been thinking about them a lot lately. Those perfect, exciting conversations that I have with my husband, dreaming and scheming about our next adventure; when we are enthusiastic, hopeful, motivated and really supporting each other; smelling the tops of my children's heads while we snuggle on our big pink chair to read or talk or watch a movie; being totally alone in a kayak on a calm river; writing a beautiful sentence; the magnificent spark when an idea has been shared and is received as intended; when people get each other; being on stage and feeling those electric moments of perfect connection with the audience; getting lost in a new place, exploring the unknown. These are those moments for me. There are others – they happen more for me as I get older and figure out how to quiet my brain and accept the parts of me that I once tried so hard to change.

There's a lot of pain in the world – a lot of uncertainty. It's scary, it's loud, and it can be very distracting. We receive the message that there's some magic pill or amount of things that will make us feel whole, but really what we are seeking are those moments – of peace, of hope, of excitement, of total connection with others, of creativity, of love. They are different for everyone and that is the magic. I've become slightly addicted to the pursuit of them, those moments of truth and meaning when it makes no difference where you come from or what your life looks like to other people. The only thing that matters is that connection, the smell, the construction of a thing, the complete surrendering to a single moment in your life and being there, still and present enough to know it's happening.

It's hard to find those moments when the noise is too loud, and we allow the pressures to make us forget the pursuit. When the people in our lives do not support or understand us that creates a hostile environment for the recognition of the moment.

I really try not to tell anyone what to do – or make prescriptions for living life the "right way." The whole point of all this is just to invite you along on my journey of figuring everything out – in my own way – because maybe we are braver, clearer, and more focused when we do this together.

My life is not about my *things*, and it's certainly not about the pursuit of the *things* or the pressures some people might place around what our lives are supposed to look like. I don't know why, maybe it's because I've never had a lot of things, or because stuff costs money and I'm cheap, or because I'm too lazy to go out and acquire said stuff – who knows. It's just never meant anything to me.

I just crave the charge that comes from love, creativity, meaning. Those moments of singular magnificent oneness with every other thing in existence, sharing the elements that make up the universe and the stars. When we feel that connection, we feel what is most real and true because we are all connected. Whether we like it or not, that is the simple truth. That's what really makes me excited – and weird in the eyes of some people. Those folks and I usually choose to spend time not doing things together because our moments are really different – I don't get what I need from them, and they think I should be committed – not to the moments but to the mental hospital.

I had to make a couple of self deprecating jokes or you wouldn't recognize me, but I have a request or challenge for us all: Let's really go out and commit to the pursuit of those moments. Let's create and direct that kindness toward ourselves, and our people. We can just give love and try really hard to understand ourselves and each other. I think that's a huge step in the direction of healing the world.

# ZIE GEZUNT

---

"I heard someone say once that many of us only seem able to find heaven by backing away from hell. And while the place that I've arrived at in my life may not precisely be everyone's idea of heavenly, I could swear sometimes — I hear angels sing."

**Carrie Fisher**

---

ZAYDE USED TO SAY "ZIE GEZUNT". In Yiddish this means "be healthy" or "be well." It strikes me that a man who spent his entire life sick, who came from little and was never able to attain very much success in the world – he didn't say be rich or be successful or be better – he merely said be well "Zie gezunt." Not that there wasn't pressure to be great – but it was from the perspective of what kind of person you were going to be. They showed us, by example, how to show love to others, and what compassion looked like, and that they expected us to make the most of our talents – that we had an obligation to use our talents in the world. I felt that pressure – at times to my own detriment because I didn't want to feel obligated to perform. Performing terrified me. Somehow I have always felt that responsibility

---

deeply. It is as if I carry the voices of generations who came before me; persecuted Jews who never had the option to follow their dreams, pursue their talents, or do much of anything other than survive. I doubt myself, and I often listen to the loud voice in my head asking "Who do you think you are?!" Then I remember how incredibly fortunate I am to have been born in this place and at this time

A few years ago, I worked with local Holocaust survivors preparing for programs commemorating the 70th anniversary of the liberation of the Auschwitz concentration camp. As part of these projects we photographed and interviewed many survivors who were still living in our community. As they were being photographed the photographer skillfully asked them questions and encouraged them to talk about anything that came up. He helped them feel comfortable and they opened up about the traumatic stories of their youth. The trauma, heartbreak, horror, and tales of survival experienced by these individuals is indescribable. Their stories are some of the most remarkable things I have ever experienced, and the people themselves are beyond description. They are strong and kind, loving and powerful. They are heroes. They are also very human, very real, and very honest. After emigrating to the U.S. they became Rabbis, musicians, hairdressers, television repairmen, tailors, housewives, spouses, parents, and grandparents. Regular people who don't look as if they've experience the worst of humanity. I thought it would show - somehow though people find a way to hope.

The most remarkable thing to experience was how filled with gratitude they were. They were happy to be Americans, proud to be Jewish, and they all said they didn't hate anyone - not even the people who committed the atrocities of the Holocaust.

In one of the interviews one of the gentleman was asked what he would want others to know – and his reply was so simple it made me cry:

"Zie gezunt" he said "Be well. If you are alive you should be happy."

If my Zayde could live with this motto and Holocaust survivors can live with this motto – then maybe we can do it too.

Zie gezunt, family.

# NIFLAOT – WONDER

He who can no longer pause to wonder and stand rapt
in awe, is as good as dead; his eyes are closed."

**Albert Einstein**

Yom Kippur is the holiest day of the Jewish year. This is the day we atone for all of the sins of the previous year – formally as a community. This doesn't mean that we only apologize or ask forgiveness one day per year – I feel like I spend half my life apologizing for something. On this day we come together and collectively ask for the forgiveness of family, friends, ourselves, and of God so that we may go forth into the new year with a clean slate – not carrying the weight of our mistakes – and make a fresh start – a new beginning.

One of my biggest personal challenges is making time for wonder – in Hebrew the word is Niflaot. The idea of making time for wonder makes me laugh – as if you can set a time to begin receiving all the secrets of the universe. I used to be the kind of creative person who thought I had no control over inspiration, and at times it can be illusive, for sure. Yet, after reading and listening to some of the great creative voices throughout history

I have come to recognize that making the time to receive the inspiration does create a mutual respect between the creative and the muse. I'm starting to think the same is true for wonder.

Before I had children, I would wake up and have my coffee outside almost daily. These days I usually gulp it down in the car racing to get to work, while also putting on my make-up and making a mental to-do list for my day. I often get so caught in the weeds of the day to day that the only wonder I can muster is where I lost my marbles and should I even bother looking for them! There are so many beautiful and terrible things on this planet that deserve our wonder and awe. I'm as guilty as anyone of putting my head down and barreling through the day. The train never stops moving and sometimes jumping from car to car is all I can do. It never occurs to me to look out the window at the passing world. Sometimes catching the moments is just another thing I'm "supposed" to be doing and, well, screw you Universe, this crap is hard and I don't wanna! Can't I just watch Netflix and scroll Facebook?

The answer to that question is yes – of course you can. You CAN do lots of things and there is a time and place for those things. BUT – if there's a time and place for those things might there also be a few minutes for wonder? And not the wonder over missing socks, incomplete homework, or the greatest wonder of them all, "What's for dinner?" Real wonder – awe at the magnificence of a perfectly written song, the way the sun shines differently in the beginning of fall, or why the women of the Hamer tribe in Ethiopia participate in bull-jumping rituals...

There are many mistakes for which I atone – impatience; a short temper; overreacting; impatience; sloth; impulsiveness;

impatience; gossip; ingratitude; and impatience. But the disregard for wonder is likely the most egregious. Wonder says there is more. It is an acknowledgement of faith, science, art, nature, things that are bigger than me. Wonder connects me to you – us to the rest of us and to the whole wide universe. It is hope, compassion and understanding. Wonder is five minutes or an hour or whatever amount of time we can find thinking about the amazing, huge, WONDERful, world of which we are a part but at times may feel disconnected from.

So for me this is the year of niflaot – wonder. Whether you are Jewish or any other religion or no religion at all – it is never too late to take a new approach, to apologize to your people, to acknowledge wrongs – to forgive yourself and ask forgiveness of others and to bask in the magnificent wonder of being alive.

# A LITTLE BIT OF COURAGE IS ENOUGH

---

"The best protection any woman can have is courage."

**Elizabeth Cady Stanton**

---

THIS MORNING AS I WALKED into work there was a fitness class going on – I work at a community center with an amazing fitness center. I'm not sure what class it was as, other than yoga, I don't tend to do my exercise in groups. However, it was a small group of women, mostly in their 30's, super fit, moving very fast with very intense looks of determination on their faces. They were engaged in a series of plank/push-up/ scissor legged torture activities, the thought of which made me immediately nauseated.

As I walked past, arm fat wiggling, mid-section ravaged from 3 children, wrapped in low-thyroid function, generalized anxiety disorder, and 12 years of motherhood exhaustion, I saw the bravest woman I'll likely see today. She was not rock-hard, covered from head to toe in lululemon (I just had to look up how to spell that since I have no experience with fitness attire), drinking coconut water, and eating spirulina energy bars. Those women are amazing and powerful and strong, don't get me wrong – spirulina is gross. No seriously, my hat goes off to anyone who moves on a regular basis.

But the lady who grabbed my attention was 55+, 30 lbs. heavier than everyone in the class, and unable to do the exercise on the ground so she was standing doing a modified version against the wall. It had just finished raining. It's mid-July in Virginia and humid as bloody hell yet she had the most pleasant smile on her face. And I just wanted to start clapping, screaming "You Go!! WOOHOO!!", jumping up and down, and dancing around her. But I thought that might be weird so I decided to write about it instead.

In a world that values "big giantness" it's often hard to remember that we are faced with a plethora of opportunities to be brave everyday – even in our smallish, suburban lives. It's not just about climbing mountains, moving to far off lands, or jumping out of airplanes.

What if we just tried things that we wanted to try without fear of judgment? And what if it was ok to not be perfect?

Every single day we are brave in magnificent and varied ways. We choose to take the leap into marriage; parenthood; divorce; going back to work; giving up a career for a new and uncertain path; taking a dance class; singing a song in front of strangers; trying public speaking for the first time; becoming bodybuilders; asking for a raise; confronting conflict; wearing shorts; getting a new hair cut or color, writing a book. These small acts of courage send a message. They speak volumes about who we are. When we make these choices we are saying there is hope. Hope for more. There is more to learn, more to be, more to teach, more to give, more to be gotten from our lives.

In that miniscule 15 seconds of seeing that lady – and all of those women – working toward their best selves I felt inspired and was reminded that the world I want us all to live in is one where we keep trying. It's a world in which we give shout outs to the acts of courage that don't register on the giantness scale but gathered collectively among us all make this a more thoughtful, compassionate, and better place to be alive. Let's recognize this in ourselves and be proud and then let's REALLY see it in others and give them our support.

Here's to being all of ourselves, a little at a time, everyday.

# "THE EDGE OF THE MIDDLE"

---

"Finite to fail but infinite to venture."

**Emily Dickinson**

---

I THINK IT'S BEEN ESTABLISHED that I don't really know what the hell I'm doing most of the time. And yet – I rarely let that stop me from doing stuff I don't know how to do. The result? I'm constantly terrified.

Something happened to me at some point on this journey that made me realize the impermanence of things. Maybe it was living through my parents' divorces when I was a kid – transitioning into new schools and new families every few years, or the tragic death of my very young aunt – to whom I was extremely close, when I was 5 years old, or maybe it was being run over by a car at 16. The things that most people valued, to me, always felt like distractions. But at the same time I couldn't figure out what was of value to me.

I wasn't motivated by money, things, or moving-up some invisible ladder. This made me appear, and feel, direction-less. Once when I was having an identity crisis in my late teens and feeling overwrought with emotion, an adult in my life, who was trying to be helpful recommended, "Why don't you become a Rabbi? They aren't very goal oriented either." Not only was this an ignorant thing to say, it was also hurtful and insulting - and kind-of hilarious if you remove all personal attachment to the situation.

The thing that no one could understand then was that I didn't lack purpose, drive, or goals - I just had no idea how to turn my skills into a career path. I wanted deep meaning, connection, and intensity. People did not relate to that desire so I often just felt alone and misunderstood. I wanted to look deeply into the ills of the day and use art, analysis, discussion, and collaboration to find solutions to the world's problems. I would not have been able to articulate that then because I only discovered this about myself over the last few years.

When I was younger the outcome of all of that was deep cynicism. I was pissed off all the time and not in a productive way. My anger was paralyzing. Everything felt pointless to me. I lived with a deep sadness that felt like a hole in my gut – there was no place for me on this Earth. I was self-destructive, fascinated with the dark side of life – with broken, lost people – yet afraid enough of the darkness to never go too far.

I stayed on the edge of the middle, straddling the divide between lost and found, fixer of brokenness in others yet deeply in need of fixing myself. That fixing came a little at a time – and continues every day forever I hope. It began with love and support from the people in my life. They loved me until I was able to find my answers in my own time. They believed in me until I was able to believe in myself – and now they believe in me even more. They also at times allowed me to build walls and accept my own limitations – but we all do the best we can with what we have. Ultimately, I had to find my own way. I have never fit into the "regular box."

I recently had a conversation with someone about an upcoming project. We were talking about the whole point of my one-woman show, *It Runs in the Family* and other projects in this movement of breaking our silence around mental illness. I talked about telling my family's stories and recognizing that, though there were very difficult issues to face, there were also so many wonderful things; but to appreciate the wonderful things you have to be willing to acknowledge and forgive the broken parts. She responded that, "When you love someone you love all of them."

Why am I saying all of this? Well, first off, to be honest with you about who I am and where I came from. But second because that statement is so true about so many things. In order to love something you have to be able to love, acknowledge, accept, forgive, all of the pieces.

Telling our stories isn't just about reducing the stigma of mental illness – it's about reducing the stigma of imperfection. We are not all ok all the time. Our houses are messy, our kids don't listen, there's not always enough money, our marriages can struggle, sometimes we fail at things that are really important to us. Sometimes we are lost, and sometimes we sit comfortably on the edge of the middle waiting too long to take a step in the direction we want to go.

A friend of mine wrote a play in high school in which she coined the phrase "the edge of the middle" – it was a symbol of all those old people too afraid to move forward in their lives. It was a cautionary tale to our generation to not get frozen in place – to not be afraid of living outside of the box – of all those wonderfully, cliché, and yet magnificently hopeful, things young people tell themselves and each other. It was the first play I produced and it meant so much to those of us involved.

Today, not living on the edge of the middle means the same thing but the stakes are different, for me at least. It's not about disappointing myself anymore – it's about having the courage to use my voice for a purpose. It's really scary. What if people don't care? What if my voice isn't strong enough? What if everything I did to get to this point, to say all the things I have to say – means nothing?

So to end where I began, I don't know what the hell I'm doing. I've never been a part of a movement or been an author, or a person who does all the things that I am currently doing. There isn't school for this stuff – at least not for a 39 year old wife and mother of 3 with a full-time job. I am a person who has things to say. I am a person who thinks a lot of other people have something to say and they are not heard. I am a person who is standing on the edge of the middle taking a step into the unknown.

# DEAR YOUNG WOMEN

---

"If you wanna fly, you gotta give up the sh*t that
weighs you down."

**Toni Morrison**

---

WELCOME TO WOMANHOOD. You don't know it yet but this will be quite an adventure. You are lucky to be a woman now. You'll never have to wear pantyhose if you don't want to. No one will sell you into marriage. You can wear pants. You can vote. You can fight in a war. It's unlikely that you will ever be encouraged to wear bunny ears, a tail and jump out of a cake or serve drinks to gross, sweaty business men. You will not be considered an old maid if you aren't married by 21 – in fact, no one thinks you should be married at 21. You can read.

You can be on the supreme court, make cupcakes, do brain surgery, fly into space, stay at home, work at home, work out of the home, build a home, wear a tool belt, false eyelashes, high heels, a pink wig and a t-shirt that says "Feminism is the radical notion that women are people."

And put it all on YouTube.

You can pierce your face, shave your head, tattoo your arms. Do you want to do that? It doesn't matter – you can and that's awesome.

Will you feel pressure from other women to be perfect? Yes.

Do you have the freedom to choose not to engage in that game? Yes.

Will you die if your life doesn't live up to Pinterest standards? You will not.

Do you want to live in a tent? You might and that's ok if you are there of your own free will.

People will try to tell you that the world is the worst it's ever been. Watching reality TV will reinforce this statement and cause you to lose faith in humanity. Do yourself a favor and don't watch reality TV.

Being a woman right now is pretty amazing. Are we free of sexism? No. Are we free to point it out? You better believe it.

Go forth into this world and be all the things. Use all of your words and for goodness sake make the most of everything you can do now that your great grandmothers were not free to do. Make your voice heard. Be creative. Be strong. Be vulnerable. Cry, laugh, work, learn, love, create, get married – or don't, have babies – or don't, be things, go places, document, sit quietly, love loudly, and use your freedom to make this world what it wants to be.

Love other women. Support each other. Be kind to each other. Give the best of yourself to the world. Only wear lipstick when you feel like it but remember – sometimes it helps. Be contradictory, be real, be something different tomorrow than you are today.

Most of all, be grateful, be hopeful, be present, be what God made you – whatever that may be. You are enough.

Love,

The Older Women

# GETTING TO HERE

A S A CHILD I CRIED ALL THE TIME. It got on everyone's nerves. I was nervous. I was always nauseated. I was a mess of emotions and expressions and fears. I never slept. I believed in ghosts and monsters and things that go bump in the night.

As a teenager I developed migraines and depression. My anger, self-loathing and sadness grew and grew. I could not be as I was in the world – without paying a terrible price. I cared too deeply about every single thing and it became increasingly more difficult for me to be successful at anything.

I spent years in a very damaging relationship with someone who reflected back to me what I saw in myself – a disappointment, a failure, a person who could never possibly measure up. We simultaneously loved and hated each other and we hurt one another a lot. For six years, we threw our pain, brokenness and dysfunction at each other. This was my first real relationship. I am sad that we spent so much time together and we weren't able to walk away as friends. We grew up together and we were barely adults when the relationship finally ended. I bear no torch, as I am gratefully married to the love of my life, but there is an open-endedness that exists when you can't make peace with someone you shared so much with once upon a time.

I became very good at pretending everything was ok. I could never stay in one place too long because eventually the people around me would discover the truth – that I was completely nuts, overly sensitive, really intense and easily overwhelmed. I couldn't let that happen.

I hopped and hopped from thing to thing, place to place always avoiding putting down roots. Other than my family, there are only two or three people who have ever accepted me for who I really am – one of those people I married, another one shares top billing with my husband and I always know she has my back, and I hers.

When I was young I lived my life with a giant hole in my heart – not literally but there was an emptiness inside that made me always feel sad. I tried to fill it with food, drugs, boys, television, music, pretending that everything was ok, obsessions, changing my hair color and the way I spelled my name, and being mean to people. For whatever reason, I have never felt worthy of success. I guess I've only ever felt that I could be accepted by my family so I have spent my life protecting myself, keeping people away, only going for things of which I could control the outcome. I was afraid – I was broken and few but those who had to could possibly love me so how could I ever become successful? That would require others seeing my worth and few outside of my family had ever shown me that was possible. I had some terribly mean step-parents and step-siblings – not all, but enough. They taught me that I couldn't be loved, or treated with kindness by people outside of my family.

In high school I found a place where I could do musical theatre. I had no idea what I was doing but enjoyed figuring it out. The teacher was tough and excellent. I finally felt like I might have a home somewhere other than in Bubbe's kitchen. Being onstage, and working on a show was the greatest thing I had ever been a part of. Yet, I was not like the other kids. Most of them had known each other their entire lives. Their parents weren't divorced. They went to church and Young Life together – I was a Jewish-ish kid, who had very strong negative feelings toward organized religion, and hated that I felt like such an outsider.

When I graduated from high school, I moved into an apartment with some friends, enrolled in college and promptly began to lose my mind. I proceeded to do a lot of drugs. It's kind-of a miracle that I am still alive. I was like a balloon floating through the air occasionally bumping into a person, purpose, or experience. I worked in retail, restaurants, and theatre trying to figure myself out and doing a terrible job of it for what felt like an eternity. I remember always feeling as if time was going so very slow. Now I often wish the days would slow down just enough to catch my breath.

I got married young by today's standard and had kids young too. I didn't fully have the opportunity to become myself before becoming their wife and mother. I honestly didn't know how to become grounded until I had children. It was out of a desperate desire not to let them down that I managed to figure it out. I'm sad for the kids sometimes because they didn't have the benefit of a mother who had fully become herself before becoming their mother. I know there are always things to wish we had done differently. I also know that no matter what I do, I will never think it's enough.

---

"We do not see things as they are, we see things as we are."

**Anais Nin**

---

# TODAY I TOOK A XANAX

---

"God grant me the serenity to accept the things I
cannot change, the courage to change the things I can,
and the wisdom to know the difference"

**Serenity Prayer - Reinhold Niebuhr**

---

I CARE A LITTLE MORE than is probably healthy about pretty much everything. Some days, I get so worried about everything being ok that I become frozen. It physically hurts to be this way. I have food issues and headaches. My skin is thin and I am raw. I feel exposed a lot. I feel powerless a lot. I feel broken a lot. I feel afraid that the world will find out how broken I really am and I will crumble into a million tiny pieces and blow away on a breeze. No one will even remember that I was here. So, I took a Xanax in order to face the day with a little less agony. Tomorrow I will feel better. It will be easier. Today is just a moment. None of this is real. I won't die from anxiety – but it certainly feels that way sometimes. In those moments, I choose to take a Xanax and pull myself together.

In the past I have been ashamed of needing to take medication. I have hated myself, more precisely I hated what I perceived as weakness. Through a lot of work, reflection, meditation, growth, maturity – constant and continuous obsessive, borderline narcissistic, internal focus, I have begun to accept these pieces of myself. This consciousness – this extreme sensitivity helps me to understand people in a way that is deep, significant and meaningful to me. It helps me to be a better artist although probably not a better friend. But I'm working on it. I feel very insignificant most of the time. The things I have to offer people do not come in the form of friendship. The things I think I have to offer the world are in the form of perspective. I don't think I'm a very good friend a lot of the time.

I'm bad at life most of the time. I forget to renew my driver's license. My car is always a mess. I'm disorganized. I'm constantly losing my keys, my phone – my marbles. I'm not fun. I don't like to shop or talk on the phone. I feel lost and awkward in most social situations with most people. Without direction or purposeful activity I feel very uncomfortable.

However, I'm also good at smiling and putting people at ease. I like focusing my attention on others. Unless I'm on stage, I would rather the focus not be on me, and even then I really enjoy connecting with the audience, talking to them, hearing them laugh and cry. It's a dance, a give and take. It's a paradox, wanting attention, and also hating it unless it's given in exactly the way I'm comfortable receiving. It's exhausting always trying to control everything. Trying to grow and be safe all at once. It's actually not possible to do both at one time. The outcome is that I end up never being truly happy with anything. I really don't want to be that person so I have had to learn to let go. Boy, is that hard. I'm coming to acknowledge the pieces of myself. I'm working on accepting all of them, fixing what I can, and letting the rest be. Some days are easier than others – hence the Xanax.

Today's an anxious day coming off of a couple of really uplifted ones. I put a lot of emotional energy into everything. I take it very personally when things go well and when things don't. So I took a Xanax. Because I hate that indescribably awful feeling in my stomach and my chest. The one that makes me feel as if I'm on fire. The one that makes me feel like I can't breathe. The one that makes me question all of my life choices. The one makes me wonder why I ever thought I could handle work AND family. The one makes me wonder who the hell I thought I was when I decided I can have a life like everyone else's. The one that brings up all of the young me feelings of self loathing and disappointment in the reality of my mind and my body. The one that reminds me that I'm an impostor.

It's there all the time but some days are just harder than others. It's never not there.

All of this reminds me why I'm here – that it's my responsibility to share my reality openly because somewhere in the depths of loss and sadness there's the knowledge that I'm not alone. There are other people just like me who wake up on occasion and need to take a Xanax.

We are not alone.

# I HAVE AN INCREDIBLE BODY

---

"Don't forget to love yourself."

**Soren Kierkegaard**

---

IT STARTED OUT INNOCENTLY ENOUGH. I was born. They counted ten fingers and ten toes. Everything appeared to be in working order. My arms were where they were supposed to be, as were my legs. Family and friends admired the adorable, chubbiness of it all. They cooed and gooed at the miracle that was new life. Every inch of me was perfect from their perspective. Everything about my existence on this earth represented possibility: the chance to make good, to right wrongs, and make a fresh start. This is not unique to my experience it's what we do with children – it's why people keep having children even in the face of a world that doesn't seem like a good, safe, or hopeful place at times. They are our window into what might be.

I moved predictably from infancy, through toddlerhood and my legs carried me along on that journey. They toddled about carrying my new, little self to all of the adventures awaiting me. No one had judgments about the shape of my face or the heft of my behind. There was only wonder at the magnificence of my existence. No one had yet negatively reflected back to me the disappointment of their own physical being as they took in my physical being. There was still the possibility that I would be built like a goddess and fulfill the deep and not so deep desire of every woman on earth to be beautiful, imperfect, and without dimples on her thighs. There was still hope for me.

Yet, something changed and at some point I began hearing things throughout my childhood and adolescence that built my understanding of my body and its value. Puberty hit me early, very early and I had a woman's body while I was still a child. Statements like, "pinch an inch" or "I'm so sorry you got my legs!" or "you need minimizer bras" began to shape how I thought about this suit into which my consciousness had been born. I started to become increasingly self-conscious and developed my own judgments about what was bad about my surface self. I had glasses and braces, big boobs and a terribly neurotic brain. Every bit of the world terrified me and I was now being betrayed by my own body. It seemed to not live up to the standards or expectations of beauty set forth in our society.

Let me be perfectly clear – no one ever said 'Erin you are ugly. You are fat. You are not ok just as you are." I was loved. I was deeply, deeply loved. What I received was what we all receive – the message that we are not living up – that the way we were born was not sufficient. It is a vicious cycle in which generations of women hear their mothers, grandmothers, sisters and aunts talk about their own bodily imperfections. They lament upon the disappointments at how their feet are shaped or the fact that they gain weight through the middle. Never once, as I was growing-up did I hear any women reflect upon the astounding capacity of their own bodies.

I have always hated my legs. They are ugly by traditional beauty standards. Throughout my 39 years on this planet I have never said one nice thing about them. The best thing I can muster is "they don't look too terrible" or "oh they don't look that bad" in looking at pictures or in the mirror. It recently occurred to me, probably much too late in life, that this body of mine has been with me since the beginning. Of course, it has – what a ridiculous thing to say – but we often live so outside of our own physical existence and we take for granted that our body will just be there. We abuse it, talk badly about it, judge it negatively, and put unrealistic expectations on it. It's funny – we wouldn't allow anyone to treat us this way and if we aren't jerks we would never act in this way toward another. So why do we allow it?

How does my body withstand my unrelenting disappointment? Because my body is incredible. I have an incredible body. This is not something I ever expected to say. It doesn't look like the ones at the gym in the Lululemon, or on the covers of the magazines, or lounging at the beach. And yet, I have an incredible body.

My heart and my brain have withstood sadness, anxiety, and deep emotional distress. My whole self has been crushed under a car, broken, then healed, and with beautiful scars to reflect this accomplishment. This body has grown three lives, stretched to fit their growth, disseminating nutrients, building little brains and blood vessels, hands and toes. These legs have carried me through races, walked cities and climbed mountains, taken me rappelling over the side of a skyscraper, held me up on hundreds of stages, and bounced my crying babies through many sleepless nights. My stomach has experienced the butterflies of love, my thighs have felt its passion, my skin its touch. These arms have hugged and held and carried and cheered through all of the moments of my life. My eyes have witnessed life and death, grief and joy, the miracles of nature, art, love, and family. My ears have heard the giggles of my children, the gorgeous, ineffable agony of music that tears through my soul, and taken in instructions on how to peel potatoes or make a hospital corner. What kind of weird, magical miracle makes all of those things possible in one place for one single individual existence?

Through every pain and joy, and fluctuation of the scale, my body has been with me, and yet it is not me. The way it looks or the way it moves or even the way that all the parts don't work the way they used to – those are not me – they are only a part. We are the sum of our parts – a mysterious coupling of insides and outsides, the culmination of our life's work, a massive piling on of beauty and pain, of successes and failures – we aren't allowed one without the other. I want "I have an incredible body" to become our mantra and I don't want it to have anything to do with what the outsides look like; but rather what this machine in which we live is capable of enduring and creating. We need it and it needs us and that is a glorious partnership.

Let's reflect this wonder and reverence to the young women in our lives. The next time you feel like saying something negative about your thighs or your jiggly arms instead just look in the mirror and say "I have an incredible body." Because you do. You really, really do.

# THE COURAGE TO OPEN OUR HEARTS

---

"Those who are willing to be vulnerable move among mysteries."

**Theodore Roethke**

---

I AM SOFT – BY NATURE. Being soft made me really hard for a long time because the world doesn't like soft people. You have to be really tough to be soft in this world. I had to learn this over many years of pain and disappointment, and being let down. My walls were very high and I was huddled safely inside. It wasn't until I became a mother that I realized my nature was exactly what the world needed – it was just going to require me to be so much stronger than I had ever been and was I ready? I had to be.

It's very easy for me to love my kids and my family openly and gushingly most of the time. That is not a problem. What I had to learn – and continue to learn– is that loving everyone openly and gushingly is much harder. People are uncomfortable with this expression a lot of the time. It makes them feel vulnerable and exposed. Doing it makes me feel vulnerable and exposed. Often it causes people to laugh at me or stare blankly not knowing how to react. That's OK. I'm going to keep doing it anyway. Being allowed to pretend that we are invulnerable, or above real, deep human connection is what has separated people, cultures, and societies. We need each other – even when we don't understand each other. We are not separate.

I recently went to the doctor and she diagnosed me with "Sensitiveness." No this isn't a medical diagnosis it's more of a medical observation. I am sensitive. No one would ever deny this about me but no doctor has ever had the foresight to understand fully what it means. I am emotionally sensitive, but I am also physically sensitive to virtually everything – food, environments, medications, light, sound, etc. I am like a person without skin. As a child I was called a hypochondriac, overly dramatic, and other things by doctors, and family, alike. They didn't know better at the time but this deeply impacted my view of myself. It impacted how I learned to understand my own needs and feelings. I learned that it wasn't ok to be this way and that I was broken. As a result, I did not develop effective coping skills around stress, fear or disappointment. I was just a complainer. I was weak. I was difficult. I don't say this to lay blame or point fingers. It is a valuable thing to learn that the messages we are sent as children are not necessarily the truth about ourselves or the world they are just the best anyone can muster in the moment. My people loved me deeply, they just didn't understand me. They saw a child who was struggling and knew that the world didn't take kindly to weakness so they tried their best to toughen me up out of deep and overwhelming love.

I am sensitive. I had to learn this lesson about myself, and teach it to others so that the world can know it too. I am sensitive.

You may also be sensitive. This does not make you weak. In fact, finding the courage to be all of your sensitive self in a hard world is the bravest thing you can do. It's easy to open yourself up to those who you know will accept it. It's so much more difficult to give yourself to those who are in pain, guarded or unfamiliar with receiving love.

Several years ago, when I was working as an in-home clinician, I remember sitting at the kitchen table with one of my families. The child I was there to work with, had a meltdown and threw her dinner plate on the floor. The rest of the children scattered and the mother started screaming. I stood up, got on the floor with the child, met her gaze and stated calmly, "I know you're upset and that's ok but we don't show our frustration like this. I'll sit here with you while you calm down and then you can grab the broom over there and clean up. When you're ready." The house itself felt like it was holding its breath. No one talked to anyone like this in this home. Mom and child alike sat staring blankly at me and each other. Then, without a word, the little girl got the broom and began sweeping up the mess. Her mother looked at me stunned. As as child, I remember feeling so overwhelmed by merely being alive. Her mother, had been the victim of so much abuse that it was hard for me to imagine how she was still alive, one day in a moment of deep honesty after several months of my working with the family, "I don't know how to give my children affection. I am afraid that I don't know how to touch them without hurting them." My heart broke for her. So many people failed to love this young woman that she had no idea of the difference between affection and abuse.

We cause so much suffering to each other. We have so much power to hurt. We have all been hurt by others, some so significantly by the people who are supposed to love and protect them. It's easy to hate, judge, and look down upon those who we don't know or understand. It's so easy to do that – to make grandiose statements about who they are and why they do the things they do. It's so much harder to love everyone, be open to everyone. It's so hard.

That mom was a mess. It would have been so easy for me to judge her as a bad person and write her and her children off. She learned to be alive in the worst of circumstances. She knew how to manipulate people to get what she wanted. She had built a wall 100 feet tall around herself. It was hard to be around her. It was hard to see how she interacted with the people in her life – especially her children. When I learned about her experiences it was hard not to understand how she had become that way. All I could do was show her compassion, give her tools, lead by example, and set expectations for how people are supposed to treat each other in a healthy way. The rest was up to her. I couldn't take it personally. It was not easy, I take everything as a reflection of my success or failure at being alive. That's a symptom of sensitivity and I'm working on it.

I wish I knew the answers to life's toughest questions. All I can say is we all have the power to make things better for ourselves and others if we are given permission to be who and what we are. That permission has to come from inside. Sometimes we are grown-ups and set in our ways before this truth is discovered and it requires a complete restructuring of all our understanding of people and the world. That is the hardest thing of all. I did that and it changed everything. It took a lot of admitting that I was wrong, it took a lot of breaking off the crust that had hardened around my very porous self. It hurt a lot before I felt better. Now there's no going back.

I am just going to love you all – no matter what – and share my passion and open my heart, say the things to the people in my life whether they are able to respond in kind or not – because that is the root of every f@%cking thing. Be brave and love each other.